HOLISTIC HEALING WITH HEART

Compiled by

JohnLiving

Retired Professional Engineer, Spiritual Healer

JohnLiving

HOLISTIC HEALING WITH HEART

Published by The Holistic Intuition Society

Our Website: www.in2it.ca

Toll Free Canada & USA: 1-866-369-7464

For other books by John Living see:

www.in2it.ca/Books.htm

Matrix Energeticists website:

www.matrixenergeticists.com

ISBN 978-0-9877350-4-1

DEDICATION

This book is dedicated to Dr Richard Bartlett ND DC and to all whose work, knowledge, and help has contributed to the content of this book, especially including the Angelic Beings who guided the teachings and manifest the healings with Matrix Energeticists.

I send my gratitude and appreciation to Gwynne Harries for proof reading this book and making some very valuable suggestions - Thanks, Gwynne !

Holistic Healing with Heart

Index of Contents

Index of Contents

Index of Contents

Index of Contents

Index of Contents

On the next page: is the messageboard/disclaimer taken at the time of publication from matrixenergetics.com

There is no claim of copyright for the articles on the forum, and any articles having an individual copyright asserted have been excluded from this book.

The information presented on this website is educational in nature and is provided only as general information. By viewing this website, you understand that you will be introduced to transformational and healing consciousness techniques based on quantum physics called Matrix Energetics ("ME"). To date, ME has yielded remarkable results and appears to have promising mental, spiritual, and physical health benefits but has yet to be fully researched by the Western academic, medical, and psychological communities. The prevailing premise is that ME with focused attention accesses the "Zero Point Energy Field" where healing and transformation may occur. By viewing this website you understand that ME could be considered experimental and Matrix Energetics International does not know how you will personally respond to ME and whether ME will help you with a particular problem

Due to the experimental nature of ME, and because it is a relatively new healing approach and the extent of its effectiveness, as well as its risks and benefits are not fully known, you agree to assume and accept full responsibility for any and all risks associated with using ME and viewing this website. You understand that if you choose to use ME it is possible that emotional or physical sensations or additional unresolved memories may surface which could be perceived as negative side effects. Emotional and/or physical material may continue to surface after using ME, indicating other issues may need to be addressed. Previously vivid or traumatic memories may fade which could adversely impact your ability to provide detailed legal testimony regarding a traumatic incident.

The information contained on this website is not intended to represent that ME is used to diagnose, treat, cure, or prevent any disease or psychological disorder. ME is not a substitute for medical or psychological treatment. Consequently, viewing this website and using ME on yourself does not replace health care from medical/psychological professionals. You agree to consult with your health care provider for any specific medical/psychological problems. In addition, you understand that any information contained on this website is not to be considered a recommendation that you stop seeing any of your health care professionals or using prescribed medication, if any, without consulting with your health care professional, even if after viewing this website and using ME it appears and indicates that such medication or therapy is unnecessary.

Any stories or testimonials presented on this website do not constitute a warranty, guarantee, or prediction regarding the outcome of an individual using ME for any particular issue. While all materials and references to other resources are given in good faith, the accuracy, validity, effectiveness, completeness, or usefulness of any information on this website, cannot be guaranteed. Matrix Energetics International accepts no responsibility or liability whatsoever for the use or misuse of the information contained on this website. Matrix Energetics International strongly advises that you seek professional advice as appropriate before implementing any protocol or opinion expressed on this website and before making any health decision.

By continuing to view this website, you knowingly, voluntarily, and intelligently assume these risks, including any adverse outcome that might result from using ME, and agree to release, indemnify, hold harmless and defend Matrix Energetics International, and its, owners, directors, agents, consultants, employees, and volunteers from and against any and all claims which you, or your representatives, may have for any loss, damage, or injury of any kind or nature arising out of or in connection with viewing this website and using ME. If any court of law rules that any part of this Disclaimer is invalid, the Disclaimer stands as if those parts were struck out

.PLEASE ENJOY OUR WEBSITE AND HAVE FUN WITH MATRIX ENERGETICS®!

About the Author

John Living was one of the first intake of the Royal Military Academy Sandhurst to be commissioned by HM Queen Elizabeth II - in 1952. He was taught to Dowse as a young officer in the Corps of Royal Engineers.

After attending university, John left the army and started business in real estate, and was elected as a member of the County Borough Council of Southend-on-Sea.

In 1965 he went to Jamaica, becoming the Resident Engineer of a major road, dyke, and bridge construction project. He later joined the National Water Authority of Jamaica, becoming the executive assistant to the General Manager. In 1976 John emigrated to Canada.

Now retired, John has been a Royal Engineer, a member of the Engineering Institute of Jamaica, a Chartered Civil Engineer, and a Professional Engineer. His main interest now is Dowsing and Healing, including Exorcism.

John was a co-founder of the Holistic Intuition Society to organize Dowsing in the Canadian Prairie Provinces - the society membership is now part of the Canadian Society of Questers, of which he is an Honorary Life member.

His articles have been published in the journals of the American, Australian, British, Canadian, New Zealand, and Swedish Dowsing societies.

John taught many people to Dowse (which he calls 'Intuition Technology') and has written a number of books on Dowsing, Healing, and Exorcism.

He now lives in a cabin overlooking the golf course on Galiano Island, halfway between Vancouver and Victoria in British Columbia. Apart from writing books and exorcising unwanted spirit attachments, John's main employment is as a butler to Pedro, a member of the famous Labrador and Husky families.

In his 'spare time' he acts like Sherlock Holmes (even smoking a Peterson pipe) to discover the intricacies of life, which he compares to a multi-dimensional jig-saw puzzle.

Chapter 1

There is no try.
Do, or do not.

The Basics

Everything is Energy

Both Quantum Physicists and Metaphysicists agree that everything is energy; they differ, however, in how they perceive that energy - from a mechanical viewpoint as Quanta, or responsive to thought.

It is now recognized that the so-called vacuum of space is actually very dense energy - with little matter, hence called a vacuum. It is estimated that matter comprises about 4% of creation.

In order to appreciate how large is this quantity of energy, the most conservative estimate is that each cubic centimeter of space contains the equivalent of the energy required to vertically lift 100,000 billion tonnes a distance of roughly equivalent to 100 billion light years, about 5 times further than the most distant object observed in the universe!

The String Theory of physicists sees waves of energy, which when bound (like the rubber in a golf ball) becomes matter. They have not yet realized a string is like a family of 'Tiny Baby Cosmic Energies' (TBCEs) following a leader to do a dance; that each TBCE thinks "How do I do this dance?", acts to do the dance, feels if it is a good dance, and loves to do very good dances - that each TBCE is a thinking, acting, feeling, and loving Being in its own right.

They do the dances to convey thoughts as waves, and combined with other family teams form photons, electrons, and sub-atomic particles; these then combine in more intricate dances to form atoms, molecules, and 'All that Is' in the physical (and other) dimensions.

'We are All the Same' - the result of the TBCEs doing different dances at different speeds in different planes to form different Beings who have different tasks - including stars, Angels, animals, plants, insects, bacteria, and rocks.

Understanding the Realms

The higher realms of Spirit are pure thought; the Astral dimensions have these thoughts taking form as thought forms; in the physical world these forms consist of matter, perhaps more dense thought forms - and in all cases the higher levels participate with and control those that are at lower levels; feedback also occurs from the lower to higher levels.

Note that although the higher levels are of pure thought, these thoughts are not necessarily pure - perhaps the old adage 'As Above, So Below' indicates that there are problems 'Upstairs' (meaning the higher levels) that cause problems in the astral and physical dimensions.

Life can be considered a game - played by those in the higher levels coming into the physical dimension to experience a different level of Being. This may be as rocks, water, insects, plants, animals, etc. - and perhaps the highest level of animal is the human being.

Perhaps it would be correct to think that each Tiny Baby Cosmic Energy is just Heart - and that when they join together in their families and teams the Hearts form a larger combined Heart.

Leadbeater and Besant in 'Occult Chemistry' describe the sub-atomic particles (which they call 'Anu') that form all elements, and are heart shaped, formed by 'Spirilla'. This is also explained in my book 'Intuition Technology' - which includes diagrams.

I understand that these spirilla are formed by the Tiny Baby Cosmic Energies from the 'Electron Clouds' that surround the nuclei - exchanging places all the time, so that all who participate have experience of the physical plane of existence, under the guidance of elementals who lead the dances.

Most people accept that they are souls having experience in a physical body; perhaps this applies to all life forms in the physical plane - although they may be other forms of elementals, not being at the spiritual level of a soul.

If so, then as souls we have an affinity to other forms in the non-physical planes of existence such as Angelic Beings, since our souls are also of Spirit.

This realization enables us to communicate with the higher levels of Spirit by methods such as prayer.

Such communication is done with thought - and thoughts travel far faster than the speed of physical light.

Our Thinking System

Remember that all that exists has been created by thought - we are aware that we think before we make something, and let us presume that this is the case for all that has ever been created, in all the planes of existence.

Thoughts concerning a person will usually be in the aura of the person as 'thought forms' having shape and colour, and will act upon the person.

General thoughts, such as those originating from a number of people, will form a 'field', such as the morphic fields described by Dr Rupert Murdoch. *Sheldrake* Examples include family and community beliefs, religions and their Deities, and those of healing systems such as Reiki and as developed by Matrix Energeticists.

Human beings have an exceptional logical brain. Whereas the intuitive brain is a parallel processor, which receives incredible amounts of information each micro second, the logical brain is a series processor and can only handle about 5 to 8 bits of information at any one time - but it can manipulate this information to change the context and create new thoughts.

We can send our thoughts directly to any Being; these can be positive or negative, to heal or to hurt. What we send out comes back to us, magnified - so it is very important to only have good thoughts, those that help and heal.

Human thoughts go into the fields of the matrix / Akashic records, where they can be accessed by linking to the corresponding field - intentionally, or inadvertently by having similar thoughts.

Such linking is via the intuitional part of our brain, and unless the linking is intended it may be blocked from reaching the logical part - but remaining in the subconscious.

This is why forming a question in the logical brain is so important - because when the answer is received by the intuitive part it will automatically be passed on to the logical part since it was requested; and since it is in reply to a question asked, the ego (commanding the logical part) will accept it instead of trying to refute it.

By asking questions, we have the ability to learn. The more information that we have on a subject, the better the new questions that we can ask to increase our knowledge.

It seems that those Beings 'Upstairs' have access to all the fields, but since they are not in the physical dimension they lack a material brain and are without much memory - and so are not able to manipulate data in the same way as a human being.

This ability to manipulate information and create new concepts can be akin to the attributes of a God - perhaps human beings are 'Gods in training'.

The key is to always use such ability for the good of all creation - not just for the benefit of self, family, friends, community, nation, and other humans, but for all of the creation of the Holy Creator. 'We are All the Same'.

It has been assumed that the Spiritual consciousness of human beings can be estimated on a scale from 0 to 1,000 - and that even the most advanced religious figures fail to reach 1,000. I have found people at the 4,000 level - they were caring about animals and plants, not just humans.

The Importance of Heart

A person's heart has neurons similar to those in the brain - but the field of the heart is far more powerful than the brain; it is probably the controller of the intuitive part of the brain and of the sub-conscious, and the link to 'Upstairs' and the fields of the matrix and Akashic records.

I like to think that each chakra, each organ, and in fact each cell of the body is commanded by an 'elemental' of various degree, each a Being in its own right, and each having Heart - and this includes our Spirit as a high level elemental, our conscious self.

I have had great success in talking to them! I do this by imagining that each is a separate person within me - and speak to them, using thought, as if they were individuals.

In many cases the elemental commanding our logical brain (our ego) is fighting the other senior elementals who command our subconscious, our Assemblage Beam (explained later) and our Heart.

This is a waste of effort - it is most important to have all the elementals working together as a good, co-ordinated team doing the best for all in our 'total Being'.

You are captain of your 'Ship of Being' - so it is up to you to get all the officers and crew working together for the good of all. You do not do this by by-passing one's ego - but by getting ego to be a good companion of the heart, since they both have the same job to do, to help your 'Ship of Being' to sail safely through the oceans of life to reach safe harbour.

A good start is tell all the elementals in your Being that you love them, and send them your thanks and gratitude for all that they are achieving together as a good team.

Practice forming questions in your logical brain, and then asking your heart (as a separate being!) for the answer. These can be similar to "If I knew (*how to change something or get some information*) what would the correct answer be?"

Awareness

Dr Frank Kinslow is a Chiropractor and author who has developed a system of working with your heart to overcome illness. His website, www.kinslowsystem.com has a most interesting meditation on awareness that teaches you to realize that you can be aware of all in your body, of all around you, and that you can expand your awareness to include the whole earth and way beyond. I strongly recommend that you download this .mp3 onto your computer and listen to it a number of times. This can also be heard in mp3 format at: (May need 'AppleQuickTime')

www.MatrixEnergeticists.com/PureAwareness.mp3

His approach for healing, about which he has written a number of books, is to move your awareness to encompass your heart and the problem that causes disease - linking these so that your heart finds a good solution.

The method that he suggests is to count up (like ascending in an elevator) to our Heart Space and then to the identified problem, linking these with the intent that the problem be healed. He finds 1 to 8 usually suffices.

He also has an .mp3 (also free) that demonstrates when you are in your heart space. Dr Kinslow's books are inexpensive and very good value - obtainable from his website, eBay, or Amazon. They include ways of using his system for benefits other than health.

Our awareness is part of our Spirit-soul-mind consciousness, and can be in more than one place at any particular time.

Thus we can be aware of our comfort, our problems, our tasks - all at the same time, although one will usually take precedence in our thoughts.

Working with the Energies of the Matrix

Dr Richard Bartlett ND DC is another Chiropractor and author who has an extended system of healing that works well, based on the concept that photons are the carriers of information. Note that these photons are not necessarily in the physical dimension, but do exist in the matrix - probably operating at speeds far greater than those of physical light.

Dr Bartlett has written 2 books - 'Matrix Energetics: The Science and Art of Transformation' which explains his system, and 'Physics of Miracles' which goes even further and includes stories of how readers of his first book have been successful in becoming Matrix Energeticists, users of his techniques.

Dr Bartlett started out as a musician, and learnt how to be a stage star. He has used this training in the way that he runs seminars world-wide - and has been very successful in passing on his knowledge to many people.

I have been to levels 1, 2, 3, and 4 seminars as well as the practitioner training - and they are great fun, but the expense mounts up very quickly. The main advantage of these seminars, from my perspective, was meeting and working with other Matrix Energeticists - I learnt very little from the seminars themselves, having perused his books many times.

At each of the seminars that I attended I checked with my Pendulum if any 'not good' energies had been removed from people but were still hanging around. I found this to be so in each of the seminars, and used my Ptah Pendulum (described later) to send them to be healed and be 'in the Light'.

Dr Bartlett has built a large business organization around his teachings, and his website is extremely useful. It has forums on the message board for Matrix Energeticists to post experiences and ask for help - but it takes time to find the gold amongst all the 'me too' comments.

To overcome this problem, I have included in this book many hints from these forums.

One important point that Dr Bartlett makes is that any one can link to the morphic field which has been built by Matrix Energeticists - and this will be explained in more detail in the chapter on morphic fields.

MatrixEnergeticists Website

There is a new website: www.MatrixEnergeticists.com

This has a few snippets of the amazing results obtained by Matrix Energeticists gleaned from forums, together with a listing of people world-wide who are prepared to organize study/practice groups. This is aimed at people who cannot afford the time and/or the cost of travel, the accommodation, and the seminars - but hopefully at least one person per group will have attended some level.

It is expected that these people will have read Dr Bartlett's books, have used the Awareness.mp3 previously mentioned, watched some of the videos posted on the internet, and that the practice sessions are along the lines suggested by the chapters in this book.

It is probable that we can organize an Association of Matrix Energeticists for those who have completed these practice sessions, and issue such members with a certificate showing them as a Certified Matrix Energeticist.

Note that possession of such a certificate does not mean that such people are recognized by any national or state authority - although it is hoped that this can be achieved in the future.

Laws and Rules

A most important piece of advice from Dr Bartlett is that in the universe there are very few laws - and no rules. All rules are man-made, and we can choose to ignore those made by others - and what is even more important, we can make our own rules.

Since we all have God Energy in us, when we make that grow we can gain the ability to influence the Universe, or even all creation - perhaps in a small way. If so, we may also amend the laws - or perhaps just 'bend them a bit'.

This applies to all the work by Dowsers and Matrix Energeticists (MEs). If you have rules that are embedded in your belief system, and if that is frozen solid you will find it most difficult to move forward.

The key is to consider your belief system like a jig-saw puzzle - perhaps multi-dimensional. Many of the pieces were given to you from others (parents, teachers, community, etc.) and you may have assembled these into a partial picture.

As you grow (in age and, hopefully, in intelligence) you realize that some of these pieces no longer have a place in your puzzle. The more you see, hear, and learn, more pieces need to be fitted in your puzzle - or rejected. You may have become attached to some of these, and find it difficult to release them.

If you can change the rules, then you can make new pieces that do fit into your puzzle. These may not be totally correct, but if the intent is good then they will probably work - and you can always make changes later to improve them, to make them have a better fit with the rest of the pieces in your puzzle.

Suggestions for your own rules

Check, using your body as a signaling device (as detailed in the chapter 'Kinesiology and Dowsing') that these rules are accepted and correctly installed to be in operation at all times.

- That all that I do is free of causing hurt or harm to any being.
- That whenever I intend to work with my heart it is so.
- That my Spirit, awareness, ego, subconscious, heart, mind, and brain work together as a co-ordinated team with my heart as leader.
- That my heart links immediately to the heart of others
  to identify problems
  to formulate solutions
  to manifest healing
- That all that I ask to be manifested does so happen.
- That even if I suggest a solution an improved solution is always available and is implemented.
- That help from the Angelic and other Beings who operate in True Holy Love is always available to me when so needed or requested.
- That when I ask any question in the format "If I knew (whatever) what would the correct answer be?" then the

correct answer will be given to me by whoever is responsible for that activity in a form that I can correctly understand.
- That at all times I live and operate in 'Easy World' - see the 'Odds and Godsends' Chapter 15.
- That I am at all times fully linked to the morphic field of Matrix Energeticists.
- That whenever anything that is 'not good' is removed it is taken to be healed in the way that is best.
- That the Frequencies will act when needed (even inverted) without me being aware of their action.

A Personal Note

After I had a hip replacement, the surgeon showed me an X-ray of the excellent result. But this X-ray also showed that my first Lumbar vertebrae was mis-aligned.

For about 10 years I have had problems on my left lower

Side - being unable to run or ride a bicycle. Three years ago I had a burst aorta, which caused great concern and needed a stent inserted. My doctor reckoned that this may have given me a heart attack, and that I also had problems with my liver, kidneys, and prostrate - plus some evidence of leukemia in my left thigh.

It seems that all or some of these may have been due to the mis-positioned vertebrae - and had I gone to a good Chiropractor I could have been spared years of suffering !

I believe that a satisfactory health care system needs to fully incorporate medical, surgical, chiropractic, acupressure methods - and healers such as Matrix Energeticists. This includes representatives of all these modalities having control over (and adequate funding) the governing bodies of the health care systems.

> Few other Beings have what humans possess - long, medium, and short term memory, with a logical brain to form questions, obtain answers, and manipulate facts to form new understandings and new devices.

Chapter 2

Thoughts precede manifestation
Visualize their shape, colour, and action.

Visualization Techniques

The following methods have been extracted from the book 'Seeing with the Mind's Eye' by Dr Mike Samuels, MD, and Nancy Samuels, with Dr Samuels most kind permission. Dr Samuels has written a number of books, including 'Healing with the Mind's Eye' - you can learn more about these on Dr Mike's website:

http://www.michaelsamuels.com/

I have found these techniques to be most useful, and present them to you with the intent that you can benefit by using them to improve your own visualization abilities.

Preliminaries

Certain things that people naturally tend to do, but may not be aware of, greatly increase their ability to hold an image in their mind, such as techniques people have used to develop the natural skills of relaxing, concentrating, and seeing.

Visualization is an inner state of mind. In order to visualize effectively people have to put themselves in a state in which they can be aware of inner processes. For most people, at least initially, it is helpful to separate themselves from distracting or chaotic external stimuli. This means finding a quiet, tranquil place, in or out of doors, for visualizing.

Eventually, it becomes possible to focus so clearly on internal stimuli that even strong external stimuli recede from consciousness.

But it is much easier to visualize in the beginning if external stimuli are at a minimum.

In addition to finding a quiet physical space, it is helpful to find a quiet mental space. This means putting aside, as far as possible, ordinary concerns. People must make a choice to temporarily put aside matters that are not directly pertinent to their visualizing.

Relaxation

Body relaxation is the first step in learning how to improve the ability to visualize. As soon as a person picks a quiet time and place he will find himself beginning to relax.

Conscious relaxation further removes extraneous stimuli, thereby allowing a person to concentrate more intensely on his inner state. Body relaxation has also been found by several researchers to facilitate the flow of internal images.

In order to relax it's important to know how tension and relaxation feel. Most people know when their muscles are really tense, but they usually cannot distinguish low levels of tension and they do not feel they are able to relax their muscles at will.

In the 1920's, Dr. Edmund Jacobson, an American physician, conducted research in muscle physiology, with emphasis on relaxation. Jacobson proved that people can become aware of tension and learn to relax. From his research Jacobson developed a technique called *progressive relaxation.*

People can become aware of the difference between tension and relaxation in their bodies by tensing a muscle and then letting it go.

Exercise for becoming aware of tension and relaxation

With your arm resting on a flat surface, raise your hand by bending it up at the wrist. When your hand is raised, the muscles on top of your forearm, below the elbow, will be contracted, tense. If you let your hand go limp, those muscles will be relaxed and your hand will drop. The feeling of tension, of contraction, when you raise your hand is subtle.

If you raise your hand back too far you may be confused by a feeling of strain in the opposing muscles of your lower forearm. If you don't feel the upper forearm tension at first, alternately raise your hand in a slow, even motion and then let it go limp. You might even rest the fingers of your other hand lightly on top of your forearm in order to feel the muscle contract under your fingers.

People can use exercises similar to the one above to become aware of tension and relaxation in any muscle in their body. In progressive relaxation. Jacobson has people work on different areas of their body, one by one, contracting muscles, letting them go, and then letting their whole body relax, for about an hour.

For most people the muscles with the greatest residual tension are those of the face and neck, especially those around the eyes and jaw. These are the muscles associated with speech and vision.

Jacobson found that when people see something in their mind's eye, there is measurable tension in their eye muscles. In fact, if people imagine a dog running from right to left, their eyes will shift from right to left.

Likewise, Jacobson found that when people think in words (inner speech) there is measurable tension in the muscles of speech, especially in the tongue and the muscles of the jaw.

When people are totally relaxed their jaw actually drops loosely and their eyes become motionless. Jacobson believes that when the body is totally relaxed, there are no images in the mind; at that moment the mind is essentially clear. He believes that the mind becomes relaxed and clear naturally as the body becomes more deeply relaxed.

It's not doing the exercises which is most important in the Jacobson method; it's allowing oneself to relax and remain relaxed. This concept of *allowing* relaxation to take place is an important one.

Emil Coue, a famous French pharmacist who wrote on the power of suggestion in the 19th century, pointed out what he called the law of reversed effort: "To make good suggestions it is absolutely necessary to do it without effort . . . the use of the will . . . must be entirely put aside. One must have recourse exclusively to the imagination." This is similar to the effect that Zen philosophers have referred to as 'letting go'.

Another commonly used technique for achieving body relaxation involves autosuggestion. It consists basically of a set of verbal instructions. People mentally repeat the instructions and *allow* the suggestions to work by themselves. The basic principle of autosuggestion is that people's bodies respond to ideas held in their mind.

Repeated inner speech is a simple way for people to hold an idea in their mind. The concept of people giving themselves a set of instructions through inner speech is fundamental to directing inner processes; the instructions don't have to be memorized, but people need to have a sense of their meaning in words best suited to themselves, which they can repeat internally.

In John Lilly's terms, what people are doing is programming their own bio-computers. They are giving themselves a set of instructions in order to accomplish a particular goal.

Relaxation exercise that uses autosuggestion:

Find a tranquil place where you won't be disturbed. Lie down with your legs uncrossed and your arms at your sides. Close your eyes, inhale slowly and deeply. Pause a moment. Then exhale slowly and completely. Allow your abdomen to rise and fall as you breathe. Do this several times. You now feel calm, comfortable, and more relaxed.

As you relax, your breathing will become slow and even. Mentally say to yourself, "My feet are relaxing. They are becoming more and more relaxed. My feet feel heavy." Rest for a moment. Repeat the same suggestions for your ankles. Rest again. In the same way, relax your lower legs, then your thighs, pausing to feel the sensations of relaxation in your muscles. Relax your pelvis. Rest. Relax your abdomen. Rest. Relax the muscles of your back. Rest. Relax your chest. Rest. Relax your fingers. Relax your hands. Rest. Relax your forearms, your upper arms, your shoulders. Rest. Relax your neck. Rest. Relax your jaw, allowing it to drop. Relax your tongue. Relax your cheeks. Relax your eyes. Rest. Relax your forehead and the top of your head. Now just rest. Allow your whole body to relax.

You are now in a calm, relaxed state of being. You can deepen this state by counting backwards. Breathe in; as you exhale slowly, say to yourself, "Ten. I am feeling very relaxed . . ." Inhale again, and as you exhale, repeat mentally, "Nine. I am feeling more relaxed . ." Breathe. "Eight. I am feeling even more relaxed . . ." "Seven. Deeper and more relaxed . . ." "Six. Even more . . ." Five (pause). Four (pause). Three (pause). Two (pause). One (pause). Zero (pause).

You are now at a deeper and more relaxed level of awareness, a level at which your body feels healthy, your mind feels peaceful and open. It is a level at which you can experience images in your mind more clearly and vividly than ever before. You can stay in this relaxed state as long as you like. To return to your ordinary consciousness, mentally say, "I am now going to move. When I count to three, I will raise my left hand and stretch my fingers. I will then feel relaxed, happy and strong, ready to continue my everyday activities."

Each time people relax, by any method, they find it easier and they relax more deeply. People experience the sensation of relaxation as tingling, radiating, or pulsing. They feel warmth or coolness, heaviness or a floating sensation. When people have followed a method of relaxation several times they may be able to relax deeply just by breathing in and out and allowing themselves to let go.

Everyone has his own methods that he uses, consciously or unconsciously, to relax. In our society, with its external orientation, most people relax through their leisure-time activities. These activities are often physical. Swimming, bike riding, jogging, hiking and yoga are all activities which, when done in harmony with the body, leave people feeling energized, tingling and relaxed. Gardening, taking walks in the country, sailing, and crafts likewise produce in the people doing them a relaxed state of body and mind similar to that achieved by relaxation exercises such as we have described. Bathing, napping, taking long car rides, listening to music, and lying in the sun can also produce states of mental and physical relaxation.

Concentration

In order to visualize effectively people must also be able to concentrate, to fix their mind on one thought or image and to hold it there. The counting breaths exercise below demonstrates that thoughts constantly enter people's minds, one after another, and that people seem to have little control over the occurrence or nature of such thoughts. Indeed, everyone has had an experience like starting to think about dinner, only to find himself thinking about what he likes to eat, then about college friends he has eaten with, and then about life at college. Obviously, if people are trying to fix their mind on one image, this lack of thought control is not helpful.

Yoga students are taught some simple exercises to help them concentrate. In addition to helping people to concentrate, these exercises also help people understand the nature of their thinking. The first of these yoga exercises involves concentration on a small external object. The object may be of any shape or substance, but it should be fairly simple and small enough so that its whole image can be taken in at a glance. Such an object might be an orange, a pencil, a light bulb, or a rock.

Exercise for concentrating on a small object.

Place the object several feet from you, so that you can easily see all of it. Look directly at the object. Keep your eyes open and think *only* of the object. You may notice the size, the shape, the color, the texture, or the parts of the object. Beyond such analysis, you may think only of the object as a whole. The goal of this exercise is to keep your attention fixed only on the object. Try to do this for at least a minute. Each time another thought comes to mind, simply go back to the object on which you're concentrating.

Practice in going back each time thoughts intrude will strengthen your ability to concentrate.

In doing this exercise most people are surprised to find that their mind wanders. They find themselves thinking about how well they're concentrating. The next moment they find themselves wondering if it hasn't been a minute yet. Then they wonder why they're doing this exercise at all. Then they hear a noise outside and wonder what's causing the noise. The point is, they are trying their best to concentrate on the object, but they find their minds are darting about - as the yogins say - "like a mischievous monkey."

<u>Exercise based on counting breaths.</u>

People who count their breaths notice that thoughts come into their mind, which make them lose track of counting. To build concentration, people just return to the count each time intrusive thoughts enter their mind.

After people have become used to noticing their thoughts and returning to the breath count, there are several other things they can do to sharpen their ability to concentrate. One is simply to stop the thought as quickly as possible, to 'cut it off in mid-sentence', as it were. The natural desire is to follow the thought through. Practice in chopping the thought off at the roots frees people from having to follow thoughts through and prevents them from becoming enmeshed in a train of thoughts that does not pertain to the count.

In fact it makes people more aware that thoughts constantly arise in their consciousness.

A second way of dealing with arising thoughts is simply to let them pass. In this approach, people maintain an impersonal attitude toward their thoughts, as if they were someone else's. They neither grab hold of the thoughts nor chop them down. They neither stop them nor pursue them. There is a Zen metaphor that thoughts are like birds flying across the sky of one's mind, and one simply watches them come into view and then disappear.

This exercise brings people to a state of heightened awareness, one in which they are relaxed yet alert. People practicing this exercise find that the quiet periods when they are only aware of counting their breaths lengthen and increase. As people become better able to concentrate on counting their breaths, they find themselves better able to concentrate on a single image. People find that they are able to hold an image for longer periods of time and are less bothered by intruding thoughts. People who have practiced any method of meditation have already developed some skills in concentration and relaxation that are useful in visualization.

Seeing

Active, alert seeing is another skill that is helpful in strengthening the ability to visualize. Seeing, as we usually speak of it, involves much more than exciting the cells of the retina. It involves more than the eye, it involves the mind. Seeing is not like pointing a camera at a scene - it is a learned ability which can always be further developed. The better people train their minds to perceive external images, the easier it becomes for them to imagine internal images as well.

For example, a man who is deep in thought might walk right by a friend on the street. If that fact is pointed out to him he might truthfully say, "I didn't even 'see' her" although she was directly in his field of vision.

In fact he did see her, but his brain was concentrated on another thought and did not bring to consciousness the image of his friend.

Another, somewhat different, example of blind seeing may take place when people view an object only with regard to a specific function. For instance, if a person is at a party and wishes to sit down, he may notice an empty chair and 'see' it only as a place to sit and rest. If someone were to ask him the next day to describe the chair in which he sat, he might not even be able to remember the color or shape of the chair. But he did see the chair and his brain recorded information about it even if he cannot consciously recall it.

The first step for people to take in developing their ability to see is to look with awareness and alertness at whatever is in their visual field. The goal is to go beyond the everyday labels associated with the things seen and to concentrate purely on the visual images. There is much more in what people see than they usually notice. One way to become aware of this is to look at one characteristic of an object after another.

Exercise for alertness

Notice the way light strikes objects: the highlights and shadows, reflections, radiolucent quality, and the range of tones it creates. With your body completely relaxed, let your eyes wander over the outline of each object. Notice sharp lines, soft lines, the total shape of the object and the smaller shapes which comprise it. Notice the texture and finish of the object: is it rough, smooth, dull, or shiny ? Look for the grain in the surface. Look at the color of the object; the subtle gradations of tone. Is the color bright or dull, faint or dark, uniform or varying? Be aware of the depth and perspective inherent in what you are looking at.

Exercise for experiencing objects.

Allow thoughts to arise freely as you fix your eyes on different aspects of an object. Try not to react verbally to, or to label, what you see.

Just try to experience the images, and the feelings that surround those images. If you do this for a long time, say fifteen to thirty minutes, you will discover a great deal about the object beyond its labeled aspects.

One of the goals of these exercises is for people to allow the object to fill their whole consciousness. This is similar to the concentration exercises discussed earlier in that the goal is for people to let no other thoughts enter their mind.

Exercise to allow an object to fill their consciousness.

Move quite close to the object so that it fills your visual field. Then move even closer in order to concentrate on a single part of the object. In doing this, you will probably realize that what your eye focuses on, and takes in the details of, begins to fill your whole consciousness as well as your visual field. Once you become experienced at moving in until an object fills your consciousness, you will be able to accomplish the same thing without changing your position, by mentally 'moving in', like a zoom lens on a camera. Or, you can imagine the object actually becoming larger and larger. Also, you can practice mentally 'zooming out', so that the object becomes smaller, and your field of vision takes in the entire side of the room in which the object is located.

As you zoom in or out you will notice new details in the object. When you zoom in you will be more aware of surface texture, small cracks, specks of dust, hair, etc. As you zoom out, you'll be more aware of shape, depth and perspective and the relationship of size between objects.

Another way for people to develop their ability to see is to look at an object from different mental points of view, as well as from different physical vantage points.

Exercise which involves rapidly shifting viewpoints.

Look at an apple. First, look at it as something to be eaten. You might imagine how the apple tastes, whether it is a variety you especially like, whether it is fresh or not. Just as you become a hungry person ready to bite into the apple, shift your viewpoint to that of an artist painting a picture of the apple. Become aware of the color of the apple, the texture, the light that is striking the apple, how difficult or easy it will be to paint it. As you become ready to pick up your brush, shift rapidly to the point of view of a worm eating his way through the apple. Then shift again, to the point of view of a migrant worker picking the apple . . . Shift once again to the viewpoint of a small child bobbing for the apple in a tub of water.

Each time people's viewpoints change, they will be aware of different aspects of the apple. Experiencing this and understanding it helps people to break free of their habitualized ways of seeing familiar objects. It makes the objects appear fresh and new and gives people greater control over the labels and associations they unconsciously use in ordinary seeing.

Exercises for '*here and now*' seeing.

Walk down a street and concentrate only on what is immediately in your field of vision. If you begin to think of problems you have or what you'll be doing after this exercise, bring your attention back to your seeing. In doing this, you'll realize that seeing is a here and now experience. As you move, the images change. All there is at any one moment is the present image.

You may also notice that qualities such as the intensity of color increase. You may find this to be a beautiful, exhilarating experience which leaves you with the kind of relaxed alertness we discussed earlier in the concentration exercises. You may even notice that you experience certain blank periods in which you cannot recall anything happening, thinking, seeing or moving. If that happens, simply return to seeing the here and now. The blank periods are examples of what the Russian mystic/philosopher Gurdjieff calls 'not remembering yourself'. In terms of this particular exercise, these periods are simply breaks in concentration. You can do the same exercise, walking down a street, from a slightly different point of view - that of remembering everything that you see. After you've walked a short distance, stop, close your eyes, and try to recall as many of the things that you saw as you can.

Another example of here and now seeing involves staring at a table with a number of objects on it. Put a number of diverse objects on your dining room table. Stare at the table for a minute, then close your eyes and see how many of the objects on the table you can see in your mind's eye. Do not list the objects verbally in your mind as you do this. Then look at the table again and see how closely what you remembered matched the things on the table. If you try this exercise several times you will probably find that you remember more objects each time.

DaVinci's Device" exercise

Leonardo da Vinci noted that when he looked at a wall that had cracks, chips, and paint stains, and let his imagination wander, he noticed resemblances to animal shapes, figures, even whole landscapes.

DaVinci felt that looking at such amorphous patterns and allowing the mind to play upon them, inventing one object after another, helped to stimulate imaginative seeing.

Everyone has had similar experiences as a child when he lay on his back and stared at fluffy cumulus clouds, finding in them ships and faces, seeing new patterns as the wind continually changed the billowy white masses. A somewhat different exercise is to find basic shapes and patterns within recognizable objects. For example, a person can look at a bicycle and notice that the hub of the wheel and the spokes make a circle with lines radiating out, while the reflector on the rear fender makes a circle on a wide line.

Awareness exercise

When looking straight ahead, be aware of all that is happening at the periphery of your vision. Do not gaze at what you see. Just become more aware of the details, and even widen your periphery of sight.

> Remember to go to Dr Frank Kinslow's website, www.kinslowsystem.com and do his most interesting meditation on awareness that takes you to your own body - and the end of the universe

Chapter 3

I am Sorry.   Please Forgive Me.
I Love you.   Thank You.

The Power of Love

<u>HO'OPONOPONO</u> - by Joe Vitale*

Two years ago, I heard about a therapist in Hawaii who cured a complete ward of criminally insane patients-- without ever seeing any of them. The psychologist would study an inmate's chart and then look within himself to see how he created that person's illness. As he improved himself, the patient improved.

When I first heard this story, I thought it was an urban legend. How could anyone heal anyone else by healing himself? How could even the best self-improvement master cure the criminally insane? It didn't make any sense. It wasn't logical, so I dismissed the story.

However, I heard it again a year later. I heard that the therapist had used a Hawaiian healing process called ho 'oponopono. I had never heard of it, yet I couldn't let it leave my mind. If the story was at all true, I had to know more. I had always understood 'total responsibility' to mean that I am responsible for what I think and do.

Beyond that, it's out of my hands. I think that most people think of total responsibility that way. We're responsible for what we do, not what anyone else does - but that's wrong.

The Hawaiian therapist who healed those mentally ill people would teach me an advanced new perspective about total responsibility. His name is Dr. Ihaleakala Hew Len.

We probably spent an hour talking on our first phone call. I asked him to tell me the complete story of his work as a therapist.

He explained that he worked at Hawaii State Hospital for four years. That ward where they kept the criminally insane was dangerous.

* The 'I' refers to Joe Vitale.

Psychologists quit on a monthly basis. The staff called in sick a lot or simply quit. People would walk through that ward with their backs against the wall, afraid of being attacked by patients. It was not a pleasant place to live, work, or visit.

Dr. Len told me that he never saw patients. He agreed to have an office and to review their files. While he looked at those files, he would work on himself. As he worked on himself, patients began to heal.

"After a few months, patients that had to be shackled were being allowed to walk freely," he told me. "Others who had to be heavily medicated were getting off their medications. And those who had no chance of ever being released were being freed." I was in awe. "Not only that," he went on, "but the staff began to enjoy coming to work".

"Absenteeism and turnover disappeared. We ended up with more staff than we needed because patients were being released, and all the staff was showing up to work. Today, that ward is closed."

This is where I had to ask the million dollar question: "What were you doing within yourself that caused those people to change?"

"I was simply healing the part of me that created them," he said. I didn't understand. Dr. Len explained that total responsibility for your life means that everything in your life - simply because it is in your life, is your responsibility. In a literal sense the entire world is your creation.

Whew. This is tough to swallow. Being responsible for what I say or do is one thing. Being responsible for what everyone in my life says or does is quite another. Yet, the truth is this: if you take complete responsibility for your life, then everything you see, hear, taste, touch, or in any way experience is your responsibility because it is in your life.

This means that terrorist activity, the president, the economy or anything you experience and don't like - is up for you to heal. They don't exist, in a manner of speaking, except as projections from inside you. The problem isn't with them, it's with you, and to change them, you have to change you.

I know this is tough to grasp, let alone accept or actually live. Blame is far easier than total responsibility, but as I spoke with Dr. Len, I began to realize that healing for him and in ho 'oponopono means loving yourself.

If you want to improve your life, you have to heal your life. If you want to cure anyone, even a mentally ill criminal you do it by healing you.

I asked Dr. Len how he went about healing himself. What was he doing, exactly, when he looked at those patients' files?

"I just kept saying, 'I'm sorry' and 'I love you' over and over again," he explained.

"That's it?" - YES

Turns out that loving yourself is the greatest way to improve yourself, and as you improve yourself, you improve your world.

Let me give you a quick example of how this works: one day, someone sent me an email that upset me. In the past I would have handled it by working on my emotional hot buttons or by trying to reason with the person who sent the nasty message.

This time, I decided to try Dr. Len's method. I kept silently saying, "I'm sorry" and "I love you"; I didn't say it to anyone in particular. I was simply evoking the spirit of love to heal within me what was creating the outer circumstance.

Within an hour I got an e-mail from the same person. He apologized for his previous message. Keep in mind that I didn't take any outward action to get that apology. I didn't even write him back. Yet, by saying "I love you", I somehow healed within me what was creating him.

I later attended a ho 'oponopono workshop run by Dr. Len. He's now 70 years old, considered a grandfatherly shaman, and is somewhat reclusive. He praised my book 'The Attractor Factor'. He told me that as I improve myself, my book's vibration will raise, and everyone will feel it when they read it. In short, as I improve, my readers will improve.

"What about the books that are already sold and out there?" I asked. "They aren't out there", he explained, once again blowing my mind with his mystic wisdom. "They are still in you." In short, there is no 'out there'. It would take a whole book to explain this advanced technique with the depth it deserves.

Suffice to say that whenever you want to improve anything in your life, there's only one place to look: inside you. When you look, do it with love.

Synchronicity Strikes Again !

When I was about halfway through the first draft of this book, I felt prompted to go to our monthly Island Fire Hall Book sale.

Once there, my eyes went to a book by Joe Vitale, whose name I recognized from the story on the Hawaiian healing method called Ho'oponopono above.

The book was called 'Zero Limits', published by John Wiley & Sons, ISBN 978-0-470-10147-6, and it told the whole story of Dr Joe Vitale working with the co-author, Dr Ihaleakala Hew Len - the therapist who did the clearing of the mental ward.

When I got home I started to read it - and could not put it down. Finally, at midnight, I went to bed, having read only half of the book - but I could not get to sleep until 3:30 in the morning - my Mind-Brain team was so very excited at the stuff that we had learnt in the book !

Perhaps my Heart, my Mind, my Brain, and my total Being were continually repeating the lessons learnt, and sending Ho'oponopono to all in Creation.

In that sleep I had a most unusual dream - that 'the Bells of Heaven were Ringing, and All in Heaven Singing' - in honour of Morrnah Nalamaku Simeona, the Kahuna for teaching Ihaleakala Hew Len, for him for putting it in practice, and for Joe Vitale who spread the word.

The sub-title of the book is "The Secret Hawaiian System for Wealth, Health, Peace, and More'. In this chapter I will try to explain the major points mentioned in the book concerning health, as seen from my perspective.

This is the sort of book that has a different, but always positive, effect for each person who reads it - being very worthwhile and most beneficial for all.

'We are All the Same'

In my cosmology, we are all composed of tiny cosmic energies working in teams to do different dances, at different speeds, in different planes of existence, to form different higher level Beings to do different jobs.

Ho'oponopono is based on a similar principle - that we are 'All the Same', in a holographic universe of some description.

In Ho'oponopono we go one step further - we recognize that we, ourselves, are intimately involved in everything that happens, that we can take responsibility for it, and that we can do something about it by working on ourselves - since we are all part of the holographic universe.

This works because in a hologram every part contains the whole of the holographic image. So we contain all the problems that everyone bears - and by healing that part in ourselves we heal that same part in others.

I suggest that all healers incorporate Ho'oponopono in the modalities that they use. In each session of therapy define Ho'oponopono for themselves:

We are all the same - all part of 'The One'.
I accept responsibility for all that occurs.
I am Sorry.   Please Forgive Me.
I Love you.   Thank You.

Then keep repeating 'Ho'oponopono' to themselves whilst doing the therapy. Remember that Love is the strongest power in all creation - Love that is non-judgmental, without restriction. I call this 'True Holy Love, Namaste'.

I suggest that we add lines to the basic statement to acknowledge that we are all the same, and that we take responsibility. I believe that these additions reinforce the acceptance by our sub-conscious and improve the healing ability.

This would be an excellent way of keeping the logical mind-brain occupied. Perhaps a connection to the morphic field of Ho'oponopono would also be beneficial.

I am doing this procedure with my exorcism work - using a Pendulum over the picture of the person involved, so as to magnify the thoughts that are sent by Ho'oponopono to all concerned with that person.

I rotate my Pendulum clockwise to do this - then it starts to make 'waves', indicating that the Angelic Beings are at work. Finally it stops, showing that work is completed for the moment. I repeat this every few days for each person, more frequently for those in great need.

There are many modalities for creating one's own reality, including healing - some work better than others for certain people in various circumstances; most do not work perfectly in every case.

A common factor in most is that we think that we are doing the work. When we do it ourselves we do so within the limits imposed by ourselves. Miracles happen when we get out of the way - and let them occur with zero limits. When we stop thinking that we are in charge, and know that we are just doing our part as guided by our intuition.

Memory Blockages

Most of the blocks to success are held in our memories, which are always accessed by our sub-conscious before any conscious thought arises or action occurs.

These blocks are like programs, one aspect leading to

another. It seems that the priority is in accordance with the emotions attached.

EFT (Emotional Freedom Technique, developed by Gary Craig) is one way of dissolving these emotions, so that although we may still have the memory there is little importance attached to it - so that it no longer affects our lives.

Using Ho'oponopono is another way - and has the advantage that we do not need to consciously link to the emotions involved. Thus when we continually use Ho'oponopono on ourselves we do 'spring cleaning' on all our memories and our sub-conscious.

Dr Hew Len tells "If you have a challenge with somebody, it is not with that person! It is that memory that is coming up that you are reacting to. That is what you have a challenge with. It is not the other person". Perhaps due to the emotional entanglement of that memory!

We do not have to know the cause of a pain or a problem - just apply Ho'oponopono to it, or where it appears to be.

Some healers suggest that we place unwanted things on our clipboard, as in computer technology. Dr Hew Len points out that although this puts this out of sight, it is still in your computer; you need to empty the recycle bin to remove it completely. Even then, it may still be in your 'back-up'. Perhaps it is best to 'clean' our memories with Ho'oponopono, rather than remove them or clear them away.

Zero State

Joe Vitale suggests that we return to the "zero state where there are no thoughts, words, deeds, memories, programs, beliefs, or anything else. Just nothing. Where nothing exists - but everything is possible".

You may share my belief that this is beyond the ability of most of us - certainly on a full-time basis. But perhaps that is the condition that we reach when we go into our 'Heart Space'.

I am also not sure that we should completely relinquish our 'free will'. I do know that we must keep an 'open mind' - and especially be fully open to our intuition, our inspiration, at all times.

Dr Hew Len tells "What we individually hold, memories or inspiration, have an immediate and absolute impact on everything from humanity to the mineral, vegetable, and animal kingdom" - as do all the changes made. Perhaps he should have added "all the Spiritual planes, all the associated morphic fields".

He says "The purpose of life is to be restored back to Love, moment to moment. To fulfill this purpose, the individual must acknowledge that he is 100 per cent responsible for creating his life the way it is. He must come to see that it is his thoughts that create his life the way it is from moment to moment. The problems are not people, places, and situations, but rather the thoughts of them. He must come to appreciate that there is no such place as 'out there'."

The Power of Love

On the next page is a picture of David before an exorcism.

A young child attachment shows in his head - due to some trauma that happened when he was about 5 years old, together with a Soul fragment and thought forms probably from a family member that died.

Around the shoulder is a Soul Program that is blocking his heart in this life.

Attachments around his hip and leg are recognized as astral fragments from other soldiers that died during fights.

Other dark shadows indicate further problems that need to be healed, having various causes.

In the 'after' picture (not shown) the darkness has all been cleared away - due to the healing given by exorcism !

This exorcism was performed by Kaye Jensen who is a most experienced clairvoyant Healer - and one of the best adjusters of the Assemblage Beam which controls our behaviour throughout life.

The images show here were obtained via an 'Indigo Qx' artificial intelligence machine, designed by Dr Bill Nelson who worked at NASA, and used mainly for stress management.

The colour of David's aura changed to be the pink colour of unconditional love.

Kaye tells how she was guided to 'inject unconditional Love' into David, which she did in her imagination.

This is similar to the pouring in of Love recommended by the late Harold McCoy of the Ozark Research Institute.

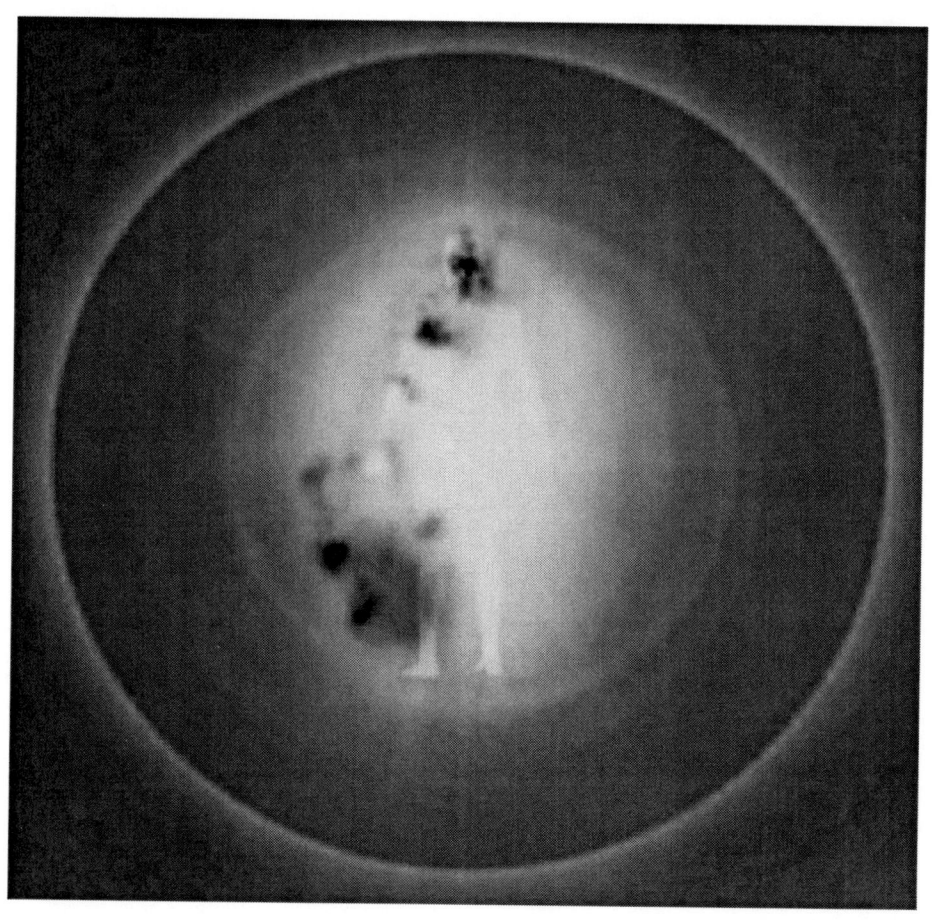

'True Holy Love, Namaste' is like the unconditional love of a parent - "I love you, but I do not like bad behavior - I ask you to change your behaviour to be good, and I will help you as best I can".

Ho'oponopono

We are all the same - all part of 'The One'.

I accept responsibility for all that occurs.

I am Sorry.   Please Forgive Me.

I Love you.   Thank You.

Chapter 4

By your Heart, Guided be
Into the real Reality

Kinesiology and Dowsing

Kinesiology

This is a system where the healee holds out their arm in a manner to resist the arm being depressed, the healer then holds a sample of a possible problem such as a potential allergy, and presses down on the healee's arm. A strong reaction indicates that the substance is not the source of the problem - a weak arm indicates that the substance is causing the allergy.

Variations exist in the part of a person being tested, and in the way the 'sample' is described - instead of holding an actual sample, the healer can focus his attention on the substance and just test.

An extension of this is when the healee may not even be present, and the healer uses his own body signals as indications of the result. This is also known as 'body dowsing'.

Auto-Kinesiology is when the healee and the healer are the same person - and when the arm itself is not tested but the body gives an agreed signal to indicate the answer.

Sometimes a problem occurs in using self-dowsing - the person's sub-conscious mind/brain may hide the truth, usually to protect the person from a perceived threat to well-being.

Gary Craig in his Emotional Freedom Technique (EFT) has developed means of detecting and overcoming such resistance.

I have found that working Heart to Heart with the healee by-passes the sub-conscious and gets the correct answers.

Dowsing

Dowsing is the technique where one's Heart-Mind-Brain team manipulates the nervous-muscular system to give a signal; it is usually used to describe the use of a tool to give such signals. Tools often used are Pendulums, 'L' rods, and 'Y' rods - each of which has its own advantages and disadvantages.

The signals that I recommend for use with a Pendulum are:

- Clockwise - YES, input good energy
- Anti-clockwise - NO, extract 'not good' energy
- To & Fro - Waiting
- Side to Side - Not Available (or not clear / precise)

These are based on the metaphysical system, where energies like to be good and spiral clockwise.

The physical system is based on whether a food is good for you:

- To & Fro - OK, a joining
- Side to Side - Avoid, a barrier

The key advantages of a Pendulum are:

- It is easy to carry around
- It can point to answers on a list
- It can point to letters to spell a message
- It can extract 'bad energies', going anti-clockwise
- It can input good energies, moving clockwise
- Rotating clockwise it forms a cone shape (circular pyramid) which acts like the paper cone of a loudspeaker to amplify the good energy / healing that you send to another.

When I am sending Healing / Love to another with my Pendulum (by working over their photograph, for example) my Pendulum sometimes makes movements that I cannot replicate myself - often they are infinity signs, with the axis of the signs rotating clockwise. When this happens, I know that Angelic Beings are involved with the work.

When I say or do something 'good' then it seems that they use me as an inverted Pendulum, making my body sway with my feet stationary.

These, I later found, were the 'waves' as found by Matrix Energeticists.

It is well known that what your sub-conscious hears from another is retained as a belief; what you say to yourself is often ignored. It is also true that what you think about is what you attract - and your thoughts towards others are also reflected into your sub-conscious, boosting the thoughts that you have on the relevant circumstances. In this way any anger, hate, etc. causes more harm to yourself than to the people involved.

It has been found (Feng Shui, etc.) that energies are very effected by shape.

Some years ago I was given precise instructions on how to make coils that attract 'not good' energy, heals it, polishes it, and sends it out as Love.

These 'Ptah Pendulums' have been found to be extremely powerful in clearing a person's aura and in clearing 'not good' energies from a place. I also use them as a form of measurement of the energies involved - as part of my 2-point process in healing.

The real Ptah Pendulum is made using tinned copper wire and is very powerful; a 'Tiny' version made of just copper wire was developed for use on diagrams - it is not as useful or as powerful as the 'real' version.

Note that I have no financial involvement in selling these.

Brain Waves

Our minds operate at different speeds to do different jobs. The following divisions are approximate:

Beta	over 13 cps	Consciously Alert
Alpha	7 - 12 cps	Physical & Mental Relaxation
Theta	4 - 7 cps	Somnolence. Healing
Delta	0.1 - 4 cps	Deep Sleep, Catalepsy

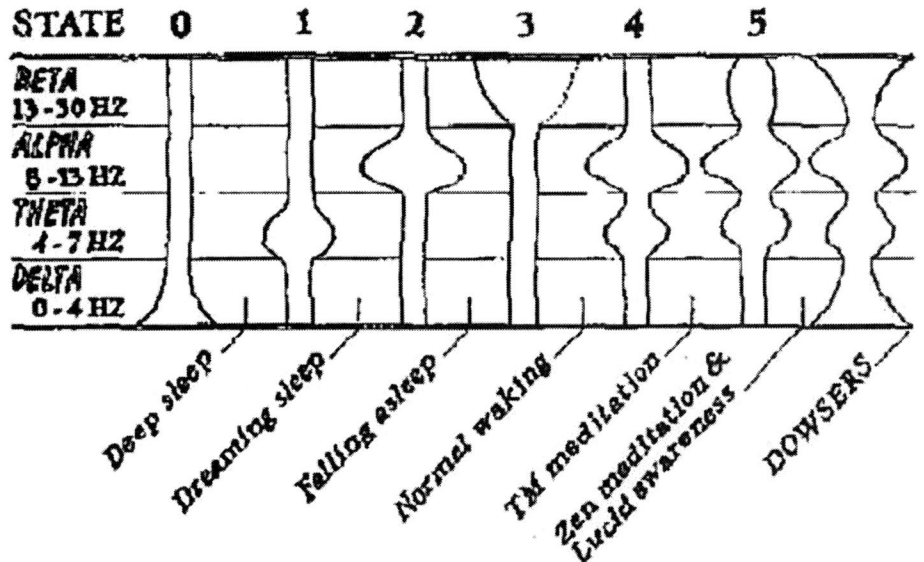

The Mind Mirror is an instrument designed in London by Dr. C. Maxwell Cade, and consists of two electroencephalographs which record both sides of the brain instantaneously.

The brain frequency analysis consists of 14 different frequency ranges, from 075 Hz to 38 Hz.

Five original patterns were established. When checking Dowsers it was found that a sixth and different pattern emerged... see the diagram above - which shows the left and right brain wave patterns for various slates in normal people, and those observed in meditative people and in experienced Dowsers.

Concerning the very high delta amplitude in all the Dowsers, Dr. Cade said it correlates with higher levels of consciousness and a reaching out to the unknown.

Certainly this is the essence of what a Dowser does - reach out for information not available to the ordinary senses. A confirmation of this interpretation is that the delta frequencies are absent in the pattern of yogis and Zen adherents, whose practice does not include a search.

The increased beta amplitude (which yogis do not have) could come from both sides of the Dowser's brain concentrating hard on the object of the search.

Your Handy Chart

Since most of us have two hands, we can use the spare one (the one not holding your Pendulum!) as a chart for many purposes.

It is best to use signals that conform to indicators that you see often, such as the speedometer and charging gauge of your car - your mind-brain team is accustomed to the signals used.

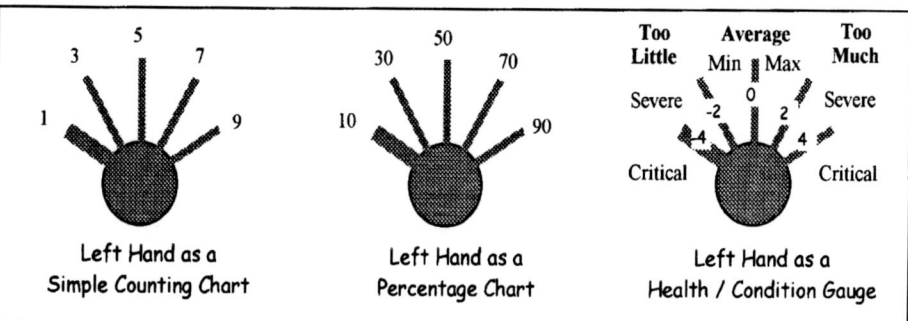

Left Hand as a
Simple Counting Chart

Left Hand as a
Percentage Chart

Left Hand as a
Health / Condition Gauge

You can use your ingenuity to let your fingers mean many different things - so long as you have ensured that your Mind-Brain team understands the meanings to be signalled for each 'hand-chart' - and that you have specified to your Mind-Brain team which 'hand-chart' is being used for the Dowsing you are now doing !

This is a quick way to check on your health or vitality, if medications are beneficial to you, how many tablets should be taken (dose, doses per day - these may change with effect already achieved), percentage accuracy of a statement, etc.

Working with 'The System'

One of the key ways that I use my Handy Chart is asking that a major change be manifested.

I ask 'The System' if the change can be made, if it is best to make the change, and if 'The System' is willing to make the change.

In this regard it is probable that the all the Angelic Beings have specific skills and abilities - and help comes best from them when they work together in a co-ordinated team, with each member contributing according to their own abilities, as guided by 'The System' as team leader.

One way of working with such teams is to access 'The System' as taught by the late Walter Woods. Experience has shown that this 'Good God System' knows the skills and abilities of helpers and co-ordinates their endeavors to get the needed results.

Using your Pendulum (rotating clockwise) over your 'Handy Chart' open in 'True Holy Love' to 'The System', explain what is needed, and ask if 'The System' is willing and able to ensure that the task is correctly completed.

Your Pendulum will start to swing anti-clockwise if 'The System' will not so assist (probably due to some problem - which you can query) otherwise start to make swings from '0' through to '10' as the first aspect of the problem is healed - then re-starting to deal with the next aspect. When it stays swinging over '10' all aspects of the task that can be healed at this time have been completed. It is best to now ask if anymore work is needed, and whether it can be done at this time.

Some Simple Guidelines

1. Be sure that the wording of your question is clear and not ambiguous.
2. Think only of your question - get other thoughts out of the way - especially all thoughts about the answer expected.
3. Remember to clearly define what you are questing, and why you are asking - and then to check *"Is the answer correct ?" "Is my understanding correct ?"*

4. If you think that you may be influencing questions that concern yourself, get somebody else to Dowse for you.
5. Respect the privacy of others - ask if you can help them before interfering, even to give them help.
6. Tiredness, stress, noise, and interruptions may lead to unreliable answers. Always check that your answers are correct and that you have understood them properly.
7. Dowsing to help others gets the best result - and gives you more satisfaction.
8. Never boast - be humble, and give credit (and thanks) to 'The System' that gave you help.
9. In all your life, only have good thoughts - always wish well for others. What you wish for others comes home - to you
10. If 'I Love You' seems inappropriate in a message that you are sending, then do not send the message.

Body Dowsing

You can define any body movement as a signal, providing that it is agreed by your Heart-Mind-Brain team - who then manipulate your nervous-muscular system to give the signal.

One signal seems to be in-built:
1. Form a YES/NO question in your logical mind
2. Stand up
3. Ask the question to your Heart as if it were a SEPARATE PERSON
4. Your body sways forward for YES, backwards NO

If I have any doubt regarding my Dowsing I use this method to check my answers:
1. Was the answer that I received correct ?
2. Did I understand it correctly ?

The following signaling systems I have found useful:

Hand Twist

Hold your normal hand out with the thumb pointing downwards; ask your YES/NO question; the hand and thumb rotate 90° for NO, 180° for YES.

Note that this often occurs before you complete your question, because your Heart already knows the question that you are asking!

Arm Swing

Hold your other arm to the outside of your body, let it swing towards your normal side to indicate a percentage. A full swing indicates completion.

Tongue

Hold your tongue in the midway position and ask your YES/NO question. Tongue to roof of mouth YES, to bottom NO. Very quick, not noticeable to others - ideal for a medical practitioner, therapist, or in a meeting!

Awareness

Imagine that your forehead is like a fuel gauge - empty to the left, full to the right. Let your awareness move like the needle of a gauge to indicate percentage completion.

It may go even more to indicate extra (more than 100%) - an example:

"Will my daughter pass her exams?" She came first!

Stickiness

Used for many years in Radionics on the touch pad - when the setting is correct your finger sticks to the touch pad. Can also be used to find a problem on a list - or a line in a computer program that is causing a problem. This is also a key component of the 2-Point procedure.

Turning

Focus your attention on something that you want to find, turn around until you feel inclined to stop - usually you are now facing in the direction of what you seek.

More Signals

You can define any signaling rules for any occasion - but they must be clear and precise, and agreed by your Heart-Mind-Brain team. Otherwise you will not get correct answers.

In each case explain to your subconscious the actual signal to be used and the meaning given - and ask if this program is accepted and will be used.

To get such an answer I suggest using the Body Sway, which seems to be already installed - how many times have you felt movement towards someone you liked, or away from a potential problem?

Remember that any question that you ask must be clear and precise - do not combine questions! Ask them separately:

- "Is work on this aspect completed?"
- "Should we continue to work on this aspect now?"
- "Is there another aspect that needs attention?"
- "Should we work on the other aspect now?"

You can also assign meanings to finger movements in the same way - different fingers indicating type of problem, source of problem, or method to be used. A variation of this would be for your awareness to go to different areas of your body as an indicator.

You can have different meanings of signals allocated for the various questions that you ask - your Heart-Mind-Brain team will know which to use.

General Comments on Dowsing

Be aware that there are questions that you should not normally ask - about your own death, or about another person.

If you ask about another person, make it quite clear that you are working to help them and not just prying into their personal matters - and this is the one time when I recommend asking permission to Dowse.

If you are refused permission ask again at a higher level, such as asking the 'Higher Self' of the person.

You can ask for clarification of the reason for refusal. It may not be to the person's advantage for whatever reason, or the time may not be suitable.

As with all metaphysical work, your intent is of paramount importance. Whatever you send out will return to you in some way, usually magnified.

Feeling

This is a very useful form of body Dowsing. When you focus your mind on an energy, you can feel it.

Mike Doney, a Master Dowser from Oregon, explained to a group of us that many energies are formed in bands, and showed us how to feel for bands of anger, of hate, of Love.

The Curry Lines, which can cause cancer and other serious health problems, can be found in this way (as well as by using your Pendulum); it is interesting that people who are clairvoyant fail to 'see' the Curry Lines - perhaps because most of them operate in the Astral Plane, but the Curry Lines are in a higher Plane, beyond their abilities of perception. For more information about noxious Earth Energies see the book 'Earth Radiation' by Kathe Bachler, available from the Holistic Intuition Society.

When feeling for such energies, do not expect to hit a 'brick wall' - their edges feel as being quite subtle. You can start by holding your hands apart, and then moving them closer together until you feel a slight resistance - this is the distance at which the auras of your hands are touching, an example of the subtle feeling.

Exercise, finding the aura of a glass of water.

- Pour some water into a glass, and taste it.

- Holding your hand about 2 feet away, gradually move your hand towards the glass until you feel slight resistance. This indicates the aura of the water.

- Now Bless this water in your normal fashion, and repeat the tasting and feeling. You will find that the water tastes better, and that its aura has probably doubled in size - which indicates that it is more beneficial for you.

Remember that this indicates the radius of the aura, and that the true value of the aura is the volume enclosed - if the radius doubles, the volume increases by cube 2*2*2 - 8 times as large, and so the 'good food value' of the water is now 8 times more than before Blessing.

- One more step - say "I Bless this water with Blessing 995 and 885, and with Healing 997 and 887" then taste it and check its aura - you may have to start with your hand 3 feet away! You will find that the water tastes even better, and that its aura has doubled its size again.

If it re-doubles, its 'Radiance' (the 'good food value') would have increased about 64 times from that of the raw water.

I was brought up to bless all my food, but when I gave up on religion I stopped.

I now bless 'all that is consumed' (not just my own food) with this numerical Blessing. I do not know what the numbers mean, but I use them because they always work, and as a result the food that I eat and the water that I drink are far better for me.

It has been proved that when you microwave food it loses almost all of its 'radiance' - and it will have an extremely small aura, if any is detected. Check this yourself! Then Bless it, and check again - you will find that its aura has returned!

Making/Improving Medicine

If you are taking allopathic drugs (made by big pharma) be aware that although most are based on natural healing patterns found in nature (which spiral clockwise) the manufactured ones lack life force and so spiral anti-clockwise; additionally they are often loaded with contaminants that cause non-beneficial side effects.

To improve your medicine use your Pendulum clockwise to Bless and Heal the medicine, sending all within the medicine 'Blessing 995 and 885, Healing 997 and 887, all with True Holy Love, Namaste'. Do this until your Pendulum stops rotating.

Next, rotate your Pendulum anti-clockwise over the medicine, with the intent of removing all the vibrational patterns that are causing unwanted side effects that are non-beneficial, sending them to be healed and in their proper place. Again, do this until your Pendulum stops rotating.

Last, rotate your Pendulum clockwise over the medicine sending it more 'True Holy Love, Namaste' and sending your Love, thanks, and gratitude to all who helped to improve the medicine - again, do this until your Pendulum stops rotating.

Finally check whether any more work is needed, and if so repeat the process.

To then make your own medicine, you can use your Pendulum to copy the vibrational patterns of the medicine into a glass of water, making it like a homeopathic remedy, specifying that it have the needed potency.

Dowse how often your improved medicine is to be taken.

> Our Heart-Mind-Brain Team manipulates our nervous-muscular system to give signals - and we can define what they mean.

Chapter 5

Your heart field is the gateway to 'All that is yet to be'

Working with Heart

Your Heart is your link to 'Upstairs' (my name for the Heavenly realms) and has the ability to connect 'Heart to Heart', probably guiding your intuition.

I use this ability all the time in my healing and exorcism work - I ask my Heart to link to the healee (the person being healed) to identify the problems and their causes, to find and apply solutions - working with the healing energies in the matrix.

This includes working with the ArchAngels and other Angelic Beings (such as those represented by the frequencies as later described) and searching in time and space for better conditions to be applied.

Whether working directly on a person, or on a token (such as a doll or teddy bear) I ask my Heart to move and manipulate my hands to do whatever is needed, similar to the way that my Heart-Mind-Brain team manipulates my nervous-muscular system in Dowsing. I become a tool of 'Upstairs' - just like a Pendulum or other Dowsing tool.

I do not know (or need to know) what is happening - no ego to get in the way. All I do need to know is anything that requires my personal action

I rely on signals received through my tongue whilst this is happening, since such signals do not interfere with my hands or main body - which are being used as the tools of 'Upstairs'.

This is so whether the action is 2-Pointing, Blessing, or inputting or extracting some energy that needs attention.

The main problem when using this technique is that of memory - remembering what needs to be done, and what has been done. This is normally handled by your logical brain, creating and using a form of checklist.

This is where having a co-ordinated team that works well together is so very important.

Your awareness can be used to enhance the correct understanding of problems, and your ego (in charge of your logical mind-brain) can form any such list and keep it up-to-date in your memory, while your Heart-Mind-Brain team uses your nervous-muscular system to manipulate your hands do what is required.

For this to work in the best way one's personal thoughts be stilled, be kept out of the way.

I usually hear 'clicks' in my head when something is removed - but each of us will probably have different signals to indicate action, depending on our own preferences.   This also happens when I use my Ptah Pendulum to work on and to clear a healee's aura.

There is one more aspect to be addressed - having the required energy / force to do the work.   Being in the physical world, we use far more energy to do something than the Beings 'Upstairs' - so it is very helpful for us to send them some of our energy for them to use in doing whatever is needed.

This can be by clapping hands, stamping feet, or (best of all) by the 'HA!' breathes used in Huna.   To do this, take a very deep breath, and shout out 'HA!' as you exhale.   Do this 4 times for maximum effect, as a completion of the healing.   When I do this, the tone changes (involuntarily) for each 'HA!' breath, the tone rising each time.

The other most important thing to do at completion of healing is to send your love, thanks, and gratitude to all who assisted in the healing.   This is so seldom done by healers - and may account for the quality of healing diminishing; "Why should we work for that so called healer when we are never thanked?" So when you always do this you are more likely to get good help whenever it is needed !

I always ask the healee to also send their love, thanks, and gratitude to all who assisted in the healing.

Getting into Heart Space

Here is a little more to help you know if you are in Head Space or Heart Space (or Heart Field). Neither place is good/bad, right/wrong. Even if it feels that way, it is only where one is, nothing more, nothing less.

Many people confuse the bottom of Head Space for Heart Space. Probably the bottom of Head Space is where your emotions are expressed. It seems that the emotional area lies right across the top of the chest, sitting right on top of Heart Space.

Heart Space on the other hand is where both the logical brain and the emotional area co-exist at the same time.

There is an interesting difference between head space and heart space. In head space emotions have an energy charge that 'hooks' you. In heart space even though one can experience any emotion it does not hook you.

In fact in Heart Space you can feel every single emotion from the most negative to the most positive and none of them hook you or even move you. You do not judge it or give it a meaning - it 'just is'. In Heart Space you are centered and neutral, able to include everything, and the thought of exclusion is no longer present.

In head space (including the emotional area) you cannot feel an emotional charge without it hooking you, and you add the meaning of good/bad, wanted/unwanted. In other words if you exclude one thing over the other you probably are still in Head Space, since an exclusion requires a 'meaning charge'.

The thinking part, head knowledge (before) stage thinks it has to be some big deal, some big thing, something totally different.

The thinking part gives the reasons of inner feelings of limitation to overcome - but that is only a thought. Have you noticed those who are enjoying happiness more than others are thinking a lot less and getting more of what they want?

What if it is completely subtle, no big deal, no big thing and not 'totally' different?

What if it were the most natural thing to do and that you've done it multiple times before?

There really is nothing to do to be in Heart Space; practice being there so you get there automatically when needed.

Stand up. Relax by dropping your shoulders and softening your Knees. Softening your knees means to think about slightly bending your knees before you bend them - when you do this you can notice your knees moving forward.

That's it, that's all there is. Simply do that, and you will notice a couple of things.

1) Your upper body will start to sway a little.

2) You will notice (if you look) that your focus of attention is no longer in your head, it is somewhere between your upper chest-heart area and your belly button.

A wonderful suggestion to be certain of getting into your Heart Space is to have that intent, start with your awareness above your head and count down 7-6-5-4-3-2-1-0 (taking an elevator through your Chakras?) and then expanding your awareness / Heart to be way outside of your body.

The feeling will be different, maybe only slightly different and that is all it needs to be, slightly. The more often or the more time you spend playing from Heart Space the more distinctions of difference you will be able to make; there is no reason to mention all of the distinctions here - it is a personal reaction; but if you don't notice one or two of the distinctions you didn't get into Heart Space.

From Heart Space there is much less doing and way more 'being' - and much less thinking.

If you find yourself analyzing it that is great. It is time to celebrate that you are back in your mind and that is wonderful as that is not bad or wrong or incorrect. It is just another experience you are having and every experience deserves to be celebrated.

Now that you are celebrating what is and no longer resisting what is, you can easily relax by dropping your shoulders and softening your knees and notice what you notice and continue the play of living life.

It is not and doesn't have to be a one time thing. It really is an on-going play experience that is available to you anytime you decide to relax and have fun with this or any serious subject that you can think about.

Healing by Feeling

The late Master Dowser, Harold McCoy, was in the US Intelligence Service, President of the American Society of Dowsers, and founded the Ozark Research Institute to do research into Healing using Dowsing methods in particular and the power of the mind in general.

Harold taught how to stand behind a person, imagine unzipping the top of their scalp, opening up the brain area, and then using tools to make repairs - and zipping it together again when the work is completed.

I do not see what I am doing, but know that my Heart will guide me to do what is needed - and put any tools directly into my hand.

So I use imaginary tools such as a vacuum to pull out rubbish, a hose to pour in Love, and I am guided where to grip things that must be pulled out, throwing them into the garbage container to be handled and healed by others, such as the Angelic Beings and other Healing Energies.

When I attended one seminar we were told to feel for cords (or similar things) that should be pulled out of a person's body.

I thought that this would be most difficult - and then realized that it was the same technique as that taught by Harold McCoy, but extended to the whole body, not just the head. I was then successful in doing the work.

Now, when doing distant healing on a person, using a doll or Teddy Bear to represent them, if I get a feeling that something needs to be pulled out, I ask my Heart to place my hands where they are needed, and pull it out; when I do this I hear a 'click' to indicate that I have been successful. I then ask to be shown any other stuff to be removed, and if so, repeat the process

What I 'pull out' is not in the physical plane - perhaps I am using my etheric (or higher) hands to do the pulling, also in the etheric (or higher) planes, in the same way that psychic surgeons operate in the Philippines and other places.

This is also the case in the 2-Pointing technique, details to follow - trust your Heart to guide your hands to the points/places needed. You then know that a connection is made between them through your Heart, and rely on your Heart to sense any measurement - keep yourself out of the way!

Do not take this as a hint to avoid doing any 2-Pointing - practice the simple 2-Point technique as much as possible, so that your total Being understands the process. Like riding a bicycle, after a few successes the routine becomes automatic.

This is the system that is used in the Eastern Martial Arts such as Tai Chi - practice the movements carefully and slowly, then when needed they will come fast and accurate.

Exercises:

Confirming signals

Stand up straight, say aloud "swaying forward signals YES; please give me the signal for YES"; repeat until you do sway forward. Repeat with backwards for NO.

When this is completed, say "When I hold my tongue in the centre of my mouth, my tongue will go to the roof of my mouth to signal YES; please give me a signal for YES with my tongue".

Repeat until successful; if this is not a success, ask "Please indicate by a body sway if there is a problem with this tongue signal" - and if YES, listen to the first thought that comes to you, and then take any corrective action that has been indicated. Repeat for your tongue moving to the jaw (bottom of mouth) for NO.

Remember that the very first thought comes from your Heart/Intuition - later thoughts may be coming from ego, and may be ignored.

Building a co-ordinated team

Say aloud "I ask all in my total Being to work together in peace, harmony, and love. I thank all of you for the love and care that you have given me for years, and send you my love and gratitude. Is this understood by all in my total Being?" Repeat until you get a signal for YES.

"We all have different jobs to do, and when we all work together in peace, harmony, and love we can achieve much more. I thank ego for supervising my logical brain, I thank my sub-conscious for taking actions when needed, and I thank my Heart for caring for all in my total Being. I ask that all in my total Being accept the leadership of my Heart, and operate in all that you do as guided by my Heart. Do all in my total Being now accept that my Heart is the leader of our team?" Repeat as previously suggested.

"I thank all in our team for working together in peace, harmony, and love for the best benefit of us all, and I send each member of our wonderful team my love, gratitude, and thanks."

Getting into your co-ordinated Heart Space

Having our Heart as the leader of our team is best emphasized by reminding all members of our team to work together in peace, harmony, joy, and love. Perhaps our team includes all our chakras - and our Assemblage Beam as explained in the chapter 'Further Thoughts'.

To do this, imagine a large ball of Golden White Light above your head, and bring this light down filling all your body.

Starting above your head, count 7-6-5-4-3-2-1-0 as you fill all your chakras - including the ones below your feet. Do you notice any difference?

Healing Program

Read this program so that you understand it and then install it so that your Heart-Mind-Brain team (especially your subconscious) uses it whenever you do healing work. It is best if each sub-section is installed separately - and checked for acceptance.

Each time you start any healing work it may be helpful to read through the program to ensure that your team does use this program; as this becomes more automatic, you can just rely on it being used - but always check that this is so.

The Program

I instruct all parts of my Being, including my Heart, my Mind, my Brain, my Subconscious, and my Ego, to accept and install this program, including amending any conflicting beliefs which would otherwise prevent acceptance, and to use it each and every occasion that we are involved in healing.

This program is to supersede and have priority over all other programs of all descriptions, but may call such programs as needed.

Signals

The major signal to be used is my tongue going up to the roof of my mouth to indicate YES, and to go down towards my jaw for NO.

Other signals and their meanings may be defined from time to time, on a permanent or temporary basis as specified when so defined.

Other methods of providing information are also to be used to improve my understanding of my part in the healing work, including visualization, speech, feeling, smelling, and tasting.

If I am not sure about my part, I can ask questions such as "If I knew what to do now, what would the correct answer be?" and "If there is a problem or difficulty that is impeding the work and needs to be overcome, what should be done?".

Intent

In each case the intent is to identify the healee (person, etc. that is to be healed), to link Heart to Heart, to determine the changes needed for the benefit of the healee, and to manifest these changes.

Overall Implementation

My Heart is to work with the Heart and subconscious of the healee to identify and remedy all problems and their causes.

Priority is to be given to root problems and their first cause; such healing may eliminate subsequent problems that were due to such roots.

There may be different aspects of any problem, and numerous causes may exist; these may have occurred in previous lives, in the womb, or at any time of the present life; such causes may also exist outside of the healee, even at the soul group or higher self levels. All are to be identified and healed.

My Heart is to request the 'Good God System' and the 'Loyal Heavenly Force for Good' to obtain all needed information and to assist to make all the changes that are required. Such changes are to be made without harm to the healee; all changes that occur shall be made in a gentle and safe way.

Healing includes making changes to the dreams, dances, vibrational patterns, and colours of all the cosmic energies and their families and teams that are causing problems, so that they become beneficial to the healee; this to be so at all levels of existence.

Conduit for Healing

I act as a conduit for healing as directed by my Heart. I ask my Heart to place my awareness and my hands where needed, moving their positions from time to time, perhaps as guided by my intuition.

This configuration links my Heart, my awareness, my hands, with the Heart and awareness of the healee; this provides a good conduit for the Healing Energies and Angelic Beings to assist them to make the needed changes.

Such a conduit is used both when working directly with a healee and when a token is used to represent the healee for healing at a distance.

When visualizing the healee the healing conduit will be made using thoughts from my Heart in the form needed. If I use a pendulum clockwise when sending these thoughts they become more powerful - similar to the way a loudspeaker attached to a radio amplifies the sound.

Since I am part of the conduit and not the healer, I do not have to know or understand the problems or the changes that are made; keeping my logical mind 'out of the way' speeds the healing and prevents me from disrupting the work being done. I just think "As I help to heal others, I get healed myself" - or similar open thoughts.

If I have questions, I can ask my Heart for answers. These will usually be similar to "Is the work finished?" or "Should I move my hands now?" - YES or NO questions to be answered by my tongue position.

Extracted from Letters sent to me by Dr Richard Bartlett:

The Field of the Heart

Is the gateway to 'All That Is' and 'The All That Is Yet To Be Experienced'. When your attention takes you to a particular space or location within an individual's field, you are not just interacting with space. You are interacting with information.

Everything in the universe is light, information, and resonance. When you are observing a particular space or place or location, you are creating resonance with information.

It is the act of the observation of that information that provides the vehicle for transformation to occur. That is why when you observe a particular space or place, things appear to change.

You are not really doing anything other than observing fields of information. However, the act of observing entangles observer with observed and facilitates a different resonance or expression of the information.

Torsion Fields

Fields of information nestle within what is referred to by physicists as torsion fields. Torsion fields are everywhere in universal consciousness. The field of the Heart is a torsion-field. It looks like a doughnut comprised of two counter-rotating fields with the inner torsion spinning one way and the outer torsion spinning in the opposite direction.

Within these torsion fields, there is a vortex. Within that vortex, information couples with the torsion fields and this creates a certain amount of inertia and simultaneous momentum which helps the information to pop through the vacuum as form, action and experience. In-form-ation as possibility creates experience directly from the field of the Heart.

The reason we drop down into the field of the Heart is that it allows us to access a state of neutrality or pure potentiality. The field of the Heart provides access to pure undifferentiated states of information and energy potential before the information separates out as matter or experience. The Heart field is the gateway to the all that is and the all that is yet to be experienced.

Consider that the torsion field of the Heart is the very first thing that forms before the physical heart comes into manifestation and everything emanates from there. When you access the field of the Heart, a state of pure torsion, you access pure potentiality before that potentiality separates out from itself as experience.

When you drop down into the field of the Heart, you don't really feel, notice, or think anything related to that experience because it's not experience yet. It's just pure potentiality. Everything that we do in Matrix Energetics, we do from the field of the Heart, which is pure potential. It gives us the access to allow for transformation to occur, because we're going back to before the collapse of the wave function.

Resonance with Patterns

We are creating resonance with a pattern before that pattern has been separated, identified and named as a particular experience. So when we work with a shoulder, it's not a shoulder - because a shoulder is something that has been separated out from the whole, identified and named as a shoulder.

In the naming of this pattern there are corresponding references that limit what is possible for that shoulder because of all the thoughts and beliefs that accompany the world of shoulders as shoulder-dom. There is too much should in shoulders and we are seeking options.

We don't label it; we don't name it. It is just a pattern. That pattern becomes pure potentiality and in that potential state there are equally-weighted possibilities. This facilitates the probability of transformation into actuality.

Your Heart and Unconditional Love

Recently I was given a directive by my guides to establish the Matrix Energetics Miracle Alliance, or MEMA.

The MEMA will be open to anyone, anywhere who wishes to participate in this momentous opportunity and its implementation is both very simple and simply profound: **For one minute, twice a day, drop down into the field of the Heart and send out pure streams of love and appreciation**. In doing this we will build a deeper and greater rapport with the universal consciousness of miraculous potential and with personal as well as global transformation.

In the past, I have stated that the field does not recognize you as separate from itself. As my guides have told me "There is no you, there is no other, there is only God (the Field I call Father)". The closer you draw in consciousness to this "undivided wholeness" (a phrase used by physicist David Bohm), the more it will recognize you as itself. I hope that you will join Melissa and me by committing to doing this twice a day for just one minute. You will gain instant access to and build rapport with the Morphic Field of Matrix Energetics. Perhaps we will all look back later this year and say that this was when our personal and collective transformation began!

The field of the Heart provides us with direct access to our inner voice, inner wisdom and inner chamber of limitless potential along with creating a connection with universal consciousness. There are no limitations when accessing the field of the heart and similarly, there are no limitations to the infinite methods of noticing, listening, and speaking from the field of the heart.

Getting into Heart Space

Some suggestions from Melissa Joy:

1. Breathe in. On exhale, simply relax your physiology: Drop your shoulders and allow your awareness to relax

into the center of your being or physical body. Notice the calmness and stillness and absence of thought. From this space, notice what you notice. What information begins to well up from your inner being?

2. Ask an open-ended question, like "What would I notice if I were to allow my awareness to move back into the Heart-field?" or "Where am I in relation to the field of my Heart?" Follow that awareness and connect to it. From this space, notice what you notice.

3. Consider that the field of the Heart is what you are. The electromagnetic field of the Heart is the first thing that pops through the vacuum, even before the physical heart forms. Therefore, you are always in your Heart. It is awareness and thoughts that move us out of resonance with being in the Heart space.

4. Elevator (e-love-ator): Observe an elevator in your head. See a miniature version of yourself stepping into the elevator and allow for the doors to close. Press the down button. Follow your awareness as the elevator descends out of your head, down through your throat and even further down into your chest cavity. Allow for the elevator doors to open. Notice what you notice when you step into that space of no space and no place.

5. Take a moment to feel into someone or something that you love unconditionally. Feel that connection. Notice the feeling and allow for that feeling to move through your entire body. Invite that feeling to center in the torsion field of your Heart and then ask it to speak to you.

6. Through the recognition that the field of the Heart is connected to everything, notice in your awareness how you are not separate as a separate body or being. See yourself as an effervescent Vitamin C tablet. Drop yourself through awareness as a vitamin C tablet into a glass of water and feel within yourself as your sense of separation dissolves. Notice that you feel a sense of dropping in and expanding out simultaneously. There is no separation between you and everything else. You are present in the here and now

and also present everywhere. Ask your Heart what it would tell you if you were to begin to listen to it now.

7. Get silly! See a waterslide from your head to your Heart with a pool in the field of the Heart. Energetically pop your eyeballs out of your head, drop them onto the slide and let them drop into the pool with a big splash. As your eyeballs resurface, notice your attention from the field of the heart.

8. Notice the constant flow of thoughts in your brain or awareness without attachment. The more we have thoughts the less likely we are able to listen to our Heart. See your thoughts as clouds floating by. Do not attach to them. Observe them neutrally with a sense of curiosity and no judgment. Observing thoughts and experiences without judgment keeps us in a state of Heart-centered awareness.

9. Pay attention to genuine desires. Desires well up from the field of the Heart and are cues or placeholders for our awareness to get our attention. Desires ARE the language of our Heart speaking to us. When we listen, we move into a flow where desires become manifestations and experiences.

10. Trust yourself. One way to begin noticing, speaking and listening from the Heart is to start by trusting in yourself. The more you develop a sense of trust in yourself, the more the Heart becomes the leading navigator in consciousness. The intellect will follow the Heart's intelligence the more you resonate in trust.

11. Let go of all sense of not being in your Heart. The thought of a problem can become the problem. Ask yourself "If I knew what I might notice were I to listen to my Heart, regardless of what anyone else might suggest, what methods of dropping into my Heart might I discover?"

Amplifying Love, Appreciation & Gratitude

Letting go is key. When you let go of the need to think or not think or to be in sickness or disease, you transcend the limitations of duality and you are able to access the state of neutrality - new to your reality.

Dropping down into the field of the heart puts you in that frame of reference for no reference for what may happen next. You are neutral - new to your reality. Now sometimes we think of being neutral as being in a state of not caring, and in one sense, the field of the heart does not care. It cares about itself as a direct extension of divine consciousness having an experience of itself through you. What that means is that it is not limited by its past experiences, by its perceived limitations.

Those are all constructs of the left brain. And the left brain does what physicists refer to as the collapse of the wave function. It consciously collapses the wave function of reality based on its expectations.

Conversely, the field of the heart uncollapses the wave function from any sort of preconceived expectation. It moves out of that expected awareness, and it aligns itself with the uncollapse of the wave function, which moves into an equally weighted probability and possibility state that is unlimited.

So it is so important to understand that your first point of reference for manifestation, transformation, change, getting rid of anything is to not try to manifest, to not try to change, not try to get rid of anything, but rather allow yourself to simply move your awareness out of resonance with thoughts, out of resonance with emotions, and drop down into that neutral state of a sea of infinite possibilities where you won't drop because there aren't any waves. It's just an endless ocean of possibilities.

The coherency of the field of the heart is actually increased when one accesses particular facets or dimensions of grace - those facets being love, appreciation, gratitude, and tranquility - the domain of universal consciousness.

> Get your Heart, your link to 'All That Is', to operate as the leader of your personal team, supervising and co-ordinating your sub-conscious and your Mind-Brain team

Chapter 6

2-Pointing and Questions

Entanglement

In the weird world of quantum physics, two linked particles can share a single fate, even when they're miles apart.

Now, two physicists have mathematically described how this spooky effect, called entanglement, could also bind particles across time.

In ordinary entanglement, two particles (usually electrons or photons) are so intimately bound that they share one quantum state (spin, momentum and a host of other variables) between them. One particle always 'knows' what the other is doing. If you make a measurement on one member of an entangled pair, then the other changes immediately.

This is the basis of the 2-Pointing.

You choose (or are guided) to a First Point - where a problem exists; this place may feel 'sticky' or rigid, in some way different from the surrounding places.

Then find a Second Point which may increase the stickiness or rigidity of the First Point, and 'imagine' that these are entangled. Your imagination actually does connect them, and the increase that you noticed is a measurement that ensures entanglement.

You are sabotaging the work if you are using your logical brain to micromanage the anticipated change before you even start.

Then go with what shows up - in the physical world or from your intuition. Notice any differences without judging them as good, bad, etc. Just different. Keep noticing any differences.

Subtleness Required

One of the major problems is putting too much effort in doing this work. It needs just a subtle connection.

You MUST stop trying. That is the main problem. Pushing, pushing and pushing until you reach frustration is giving up, not surrendering.

You must realize that the 2-Point is performed with the most subtle and sensitive adjustments that you make within your consciousness. There are no protocols, there are no strategies, there is almost no doing.

You must become accustomed to recognizing that the most powerful and prolific changes will occur as a result of the most minute changes in your perceptions.

For a moment, practice doing the most subtle things you can think of. Take a pencil, coaster, cup or anything on the table next to you and move it the smallest possible distance. Then keep doing it, with smaller and smaller distances.

Turn your neck to the left, using the least amount of energy, and move it the least amount, barely perceptible, distance. This is the same subtleness you are going to bring to your 2-Point. It's basically a finely adjusted shift in your attention.

If you try harder, you will totally lose the finesse and absolute total simplicity that is required for the 2-Point. That is the challenge.

We are trained to strategize, plan, follow protocols. We have complicated exercise plans, diet routines. Studying requires taking notes, underlining and exerting effort. There is absolutely no effort in working with the Matrix - it's a HUGE change in paradigm.

It requires less adjustment than picking up your remote to change the channel. You are relearning actions, unlearning old behaviors.

Focus on a point in front of you. On the wall, on a piece of furniture, on a book on the bookshelf.

It is a very soft focus that requires no effort. You might notice your attention shifts slightly up or down or left or right - but comes back to that pin point you have chosen. Now practice moving your attention to a new point just an inch or less away.

You are practicing subtlety and 'not doing'.

Contemplate on what you are doing by simply taking all your attention and putting it on one point.

Maybe you've heard the saying that "energy flows where intention goes".

Your intention and attention and all your life force is now focused on a small point within time and space. Realize how much life force that can be.

Now, we are going to take a giant leap. You are free to move your attention to a point at least one foot away in any direction.

Drawing a Line

However as you move your eyes, you are drawing a line between the point you are softly gazing at and the new point. You are simply focused on observing the shift from one point to another. You are doing nothing else.

Practice gazing at a cup on the table and drawing a line between another object in your house. Make that line a thread, an ink line or just observe it like you would a sunset or something that you are simply observing and enjoying. When you move from the soft point of gaze to another what you are doing is moving your energy from one point in time and space and interacting with another point in time and space.

This is dealing with the measurement problem in quantum physics.

Just for practice, every hour find some first point and a second point, and see/feel their connection - without any other intent than just practicing finding two points and connecting / entangling them.

As you get used to using subtle movements you can start choosing points that relate to something that you are feeling, such as anger, frustration, or sadness. Just pick a point on the body or in your field where you think that it might be. Then pick a second point. Anywhere. Don't worry if it is sticky or not. You are just practicing connecting points with lines of energy.

If you continue to practice this, including the subtle shifts that you make with your attention, you will be 2-Pointing. Any attempt to try harder, do more will work against you.

Forget about quantum entanglement, and the theory behind it for a moment. On a totally practical level, if I 2-Point two tree's on a hill, or a telephone pole and a fire hydrant, I indeed experience a shift.

Intention to Make a Change

However, my experience of that shift is vastly different from my experience if I make a decision or intention to focus my attention/energy on an experience I am having whether it be a pain in my back or a twitching eye.

All of a sudden 100% of my soft focus is now on that which I would like to change. It creates purpose, it creates an opportunity to consciously make a change to something that has now appeared in the matrix. That pain or twitch represents a 'story' which I have now chosen to present.

The fact that I have chosen to pay attention to it and direct my attention to it in itself is a powerful event. I am taking an unconscious message and applying a conscious decision to change it. That's a subjective and inward act, but it is nonetheless an act of my will. But that's as far as I go applying my will.

Your attention is the most important commodity you own. Everybody wants it. A business knows that if it can get your attention, it has a chance to sway or convince you to make a choice.

If you focus on money, you will likely change your money situation - not necessarily for the better if your focus is fear based! If you focus on God, you will inevitably bring that God Energy into your life.

If you focus on a problem state, you will inevitably be more aware of it and now are collaborating with it to bring it forward and resolve it. Your focus on neck pain might bring into greater focus (and even intensify) the experience because now your focus is on it. That experience is vastly different than arbitrarily focusing on an inanimate object.

But there is a 'however'. If I choose for that inanimate object to represent something then my relation to it changes. I have now changed my relationship to that object by making a decision.

How to Locate the Points

And if, after all these other good ideas you still can't see or feel anything for a 2-Point, try hearing them!

What would I hear if I could hear a 2-Point? A bell? A buzz? A whistle? A burp? Whatever works for you!

If I could hear my 1st point where would it be?

If I could hear my 2nd point where would it be?

Or try knowing them:

If I knew where my 1st point was where would it be? TRUST what you get, and just go with it.

If I knew where my 2nd point was where would it be? Again just trust what shows up, play along with it.

We don't all receive information the same way. As there are no rules in the ME field there is no reason that a 2-Point won't show up in a different way that is more useful for you!

In fact, why not ask "If a 2-Point was to show up in a way that was useful for me, how would it show up?"

I can't always find 'two' points so I take my heart space as the first and just find another. Sometimes my attention is drawn there and I just run with it - even if that is just a mark on a wall, or a reflection in my TV, or a light. Sometimes I move one hand around in the air until I feel a tingle in my fingers or slight pressure and then take that as my second point.

I find it helps not to over-analyze your two points.

Oh, and keep asking questions! "If I could see a second point, where would it be? What would it look like? How would it show up for me? What might it sound like? Would it be a colour? Might it be an object? Would it be a song? Maybe I could smell it? Could I feel it in my hand? Where in my body might I feel it? What would I notice if I were to notice something? Might I notice nothing? Does that matter? If I don't know what to do, what might I do?"

Give the universe a chance to answer in between your asking of questions - and notice if any of your questions draw your attention to something.

If you can't find the second point, let the second point come to you. Extend your second hand and just KNOW that the point will be there. If you sense a small or large shift in your first point, consider that your second point. I like to think of it as the two points 'talking' to each other. At that juncture, acknowledge. then let go - or do what comes to you intuitively.

Using the 2-Point Technique

The key to using a 2-Point technique is letting it go. You must release it to the matrix before it can have any effect. It is not you who is doing the work to make a change.

One way to look at a 2-Point is to imagine that since they are now connected there is now a wave between the two points that carries information - with the intent that the better information will prevail over that which is causing problems.

In other words you are collapsing the 'not wanted' wave of information, and replacing it with a new wave that initiates the change.

You can imagine the wave being like a radio communication, but at the speed of thought - many times faster than that of any electro-magnetic signal in the physical plane, probably the square of speed in the physical plane, or even higher, carried via the matrix.

You are not bringing the energy-matter from one to the other, but changing the dances / vibrational patterns that are made from 'problematic' to 'improved'. Hence you will not have any adverse effect on the source of the improved pattern.

If the cosmos is holographic, then it may be that your action in releasing the 2-Point makes a change in the source of the hologram - of which you would be a part; thus future holographic emanations from the source would continue to be as 'improved', unless (and until) some further action occurred that made a different change.

Letting Go

How do you let the 2-Point go? Just say 'Go!', and perhaps imagine the change being implemented as you intended - not watching for change or micro-management, but being aware of any changes that do occur.

Do not make things complicated - that is 'screwing up'. The process is very simple - like child's play. Keep it that way - simple and easy to do, without any ego involvement.

You do not have to understand 'how' it works - just 'know' that it does! If you have any problems, check that you are working from your Heart space, and link to the morphic field built by all the other Matrix Energeticists, asking for the help needed, and be guided by the response:

"If I knew what to do, what would the correct answer be?"

Questions

One of the biggest and most important lessons to be learnt is to keep an open mind. This also implies that we do NOT 'Know it All', together with a realization that we can get help by asking questions.

This is most easily accomplished when we ask from our Heart Space.

Here are a few suggestions for the sort of questions that will help you, not only when working with the Matrix, but also in every aspect of your life.

Most of these are formulated for your own use - amend them to suit your needs, or fit another person that is your client, etc.

- If I knew the best way to express my intent, what would the correct answer be?
- If I knew where the first (or second) point is, where would it be?
- If I knew where to place my hands, where would they go?
- If my Heart knew where to place my hands, where would they be put?
- If I knew how to let this 2-Point go, what would I do?
- What is the most useful question that I can ask?
- If I were to understand how to do it, what would it look like? Feel like? Example: Collapse the wave.
- If I access new possibilities, which will give the most benefit?
- How will this be useful and beneficial?
- Have I finished the present work? Is more work needed in the future?
- Which modality will be the best to use?
- Am I willing to believe that it is easy to do?
- Do I need to do the 2 point, or is it already done?
- How can I embrace creative potential?

- If I harmonize myself in relation to finances, how would I like that to be?
- If I have doubt, which part do I want to doubt first?
- How can I be flexible in my noticing/observing?
- How can I have fun in my noticing?
- How can I notice and see more clearly?
- How can I step outside of and notice the noticer?
- What is the meaning of that dream?
- Is there a lesson to be learnt from that dream?
- Is there a lesson to be learnt from that situation?
- How could I shift my intent?
- How do I do it now?
- What do I need to do next?
- How do I pop into the grid? Ask!
- Where would I like that energy to be?
- How is this situation serving me?
- Is this being caused by my sub-conscious to protect me?
- Is this protection still needed?
- How is this helping me grow?
- By transcending this, how can I help myself and others?
- In what way can I notice now what I haven't yet noticed that helps me and mankind?
- How can I return to pure intent and let it guide me throughout the day?
- What do I do next?
- If X were to have the experience, where would my attention go?
- If I did have an opening, what would it be?
- If I did see something, what would it be?
- If I do not feel that I got what I wanted, where can I go to get It?
- If I were to have a symbol which would activate a deeply desired state, for my and others highest good, what would it be?

- How would it feel if it had already activated?
- If this would be different, what would it be like? If we were to do more ...., what do I notice?
- If you are not this body, who are you?
- If I could see in color, what would I see ?
- If I were to notice something, what would it be? look/sound/feel like?
- What information has this symbol to give me?
- Do I need to integrate something?
- What do I notice?
- What gets my attention?
- What is good about this?
- Who knows what will be important?
- Why not imagine that it is gone?
- Why not make stupid beliefs useful?
- If I could improve my life [skills, abilities, wealth, etc.], what would I do? Do now? Do today?
- What am I not now noticing that if I did notice it would be of use and assistance to me?
- What completely new thought would advance me?
- What am I missing, not noticing?
- How can I be more child-like in my thinking, make this more fun - for me and those who help me?

Some Thoughts - for Meditation!

- You don't have to hold the thought. Accept it now. "That's OK" releases the judgment. Now we have a choice.
- The act of observing causes change.
- The charged potential of my thoughts is enough to pop it through.
- The easy way is the best way.
- The less I do, the more happens.
- The less I know, and the more confused I am, the more powerful I am, and better the work that I do.

- The less I know, the more amazing my results.
- The less I do, the more possibilities there are, more powerful the outcomes.
- The less you know/analyze, the better.
- The less you try/do, the more you have.
- The more ridiculous it is, the more I let go and have fun, the less I take seriously, the more powerful my work.
- The need to do something, to be powerful, keeps us from it.
- The Universe shows up when I play.
- The way we observe causes it to collapse into our expectations Expect to see nothing, and the other possibility shows up.
- The whole universe listens to you.
- There are no wrong answers.
- Things are not things, they are perceptions.
- Things can change without anything occurring.
- Things easily pop out of the vacuum of zero point, a seething sea of energy.
- Trust that a spinning wheel [a symbol showing up] will be useful.
- Drop down in heart place, define intent, let go.
- Trust that something is happening.
- Where attention goes, energy flows.
- Weak measurement: Let go and get out of the way; do as little as possible. It allows for information and shift, collapses possible into actuality
- What I intend and think creates reality, doesn't block what happens.
- What we try to avoid most - happens.
- Whatever happens is grace - anything can happen.
- Whatever shows up as I play may change the rules of the game for the better.
- Whatever shows up is perfect in the moment,

unbidden, unexpected, surprising - and useful .
- Whatever shows up shows up, may seem unrelated.
- Whatever shows up, I get interested in it.
- Whatever thought came up, use it.
- When heart says do, do.
- When I don't like the game I change the rules.
- When I give up control, great stuff shows up.
- When I look at it, I allow it to just be.
- When I play, deep, permanent change happens .
- When I stop looking at it, it goes back to the wave, and reassembles itself.
- When in zero point, I have access to anything I want.
- When you encounter any limit, change the rules.
- You need less than a blink for massive change.
- Your greatest fear holds your greatest gift.

Practice 2-Pointing ALL the time to improve your skill - no large effort, but enormous trust, knowing that it works, and noticing what is different.

Chapter 7

To a Morphic Field you link
To Improve the way you Think

The Matrix, Fields, and Forms

Grid Lines

Mike Doney, a very experienced Dowser, explained at a convention that many energies run in grid lines; he taught us to feel for bands of different energies, such as colours (red, blue, yellow, etc.), emotions (greed, love, fear, etc.), as well as the earth energies that run in the Currie Grid (NE-SW & NW-SE) and Hartmann Grid (NS & EW) - both the latter named after medical doctors in Germany who discovered their noxious energies associated with cancer and other diseases.

Clairvoyants can see the Hartmann Grid, but not the Currie grid, since it seems to be in a plane higher than they can access. The Hartmann grid is usually beneficial, except when it has been polluted by EMF due to unbalanced returns of electrical energy, especially in rural areas.

Mike's method is for us to have the intent to locate the band that carries a chosen energy, and then to walk in any direction holding the palm of our hand open until our hand meets a slight resistance - in the same way that we checked for auras of water (and of food, animals, plants, or people) in a previous exercise.

Having marked the spot where resistance was felt, we moved to a few more spots to determine the direction and width of the energy band, and the spacing between bands - including the bands at right angles to the band that was first found. Parallel bands are found to have alternating directions (the Hartmann grid would run N to S, then S to N; these being crossed by bands alternating E to W and W to E.

When dealing with these earth energy grids it is found that they originate in the earth and extend upwards without loss of strength to the top of very high buildings.

It seems that these bands spread out to diffuse the emotions that they carry - and in doing so, cause these emotions to resonate in people who are close to the source. Examples are fans at sport events, attendees at political or religious meetings.

Vivaxis

The late Frances Nixon discovered that all humans have a personal grid, the prime 'ray' aimed at their 'Vivaxis', usually located at their place of birth, with secondary rays reversed and at right angles to the prime ray - all of which can be used to communicate.

It seems that the Vivaxis holds the Akashic record of a person whilst they are alive in a physical body. Once you have had any contact with another person, their identity and Vivaxis is stored in an 'address book' in your memory.

Whenever you think of such a person, your mind looks up their Vivaxis/address, gets feedback about the person's current location, and then sends your thoughts directly to the person.

The late William Wilks went further; he found that all forms have a Vivaxis - he could identify where a carrot was grown, a gold nugget formed, or a piece of jewellery was made. If the form was subjected to any intense blast of energy, such as a nugget being melted or a carrot being consumed, a new Vivaxis was formed where the change occurred.

Thus a person spending a lot of time in a vortex of energy (such as crossings of powerful noxious energies or X-rays) could suffer from the body cells so exposed getting a new Vivaxis - differing from that of the rest of their body, and so not responding in the same way to various influences.

Hence the affected cells are 'out of control' and diseases may occur, such as cancer. As Käthe Bachler reports, many children are very sensitive to noxious energies, and may avoid areas of their cots which are so exposed.

There have been occasions when a healthy baby has been left in very powerful energies for 30 minutes and died; these noxious energies are probably responsible for most sudden deaths of infants.

The grids mentioned above are mainly in the vertical plane - some Dowsers have located bands of energies that are horizontal; more information is scarce. It may be that these are the lines of thought propagated by human beings, which are then seeking bands of energy with which to resonate; it is possible that curses may be included in this category.

These grids seem to be earth-centered. Based on the precept 'As Above, So Below' it can be assumed that there are higher levels of grids that form a matrix in the heavens.

Morphic Fields

These are not flat areas like those cultivated by farmers, but more similar to clouds having three dimensions - although even more dimensions may be involved. Such clouds can interpenetrate each other and be of various strengths and sizes, being non-material regions of influence, extending in space and time.

Morphic, or form-conveying fields, are non-material regions of influence, extending in space and continuing in time, localized within and around the systems they organize.

I know that didn't sound so simple but basically what they are saying is that everything has a set of experiences in nature - a pattern of existence both past and present. A collection of all of these patterns of existence, both action and interaction, is what forms a morphic field. You can think of morphic fields as a library with the cumulative memory of every pattern of existence of a person or item.

An individual will have his own auric field, interpenetrated by the fields of others in the family, community, and nation. There will be fields representing belief systems, professional/trade skills, artistic/recreational interests, and social/religious affiliations.

These are sets of experiences - patterns of existence from both past and present.

Thus a field can become a 'morphic field' when you resonate with it (intentionally or by chance) as postulated by Dr Rupert ~~Murdoch~~. *Sheldrake.*

The fields to which a person resonates will have far greater influences than the non-resonant fields, even if those are larger and stronger.

Morphic Resonance

Morphic resonance is the process that allows the information contained in morphic fields to act upon an individual or an item.

In this work we are concerned with linking by intent to fields that are desired for overall benefit.

All the knowledge that has ever existed in the cosmos remains in such fields. Your Heart is the key to working with 'Upstairs' (my word for the non-physical realms) so by forming open questions with your left/logical brain ("If I knew about xxxx, what would I know?") and asking your Heart to obtain the answer, it will appear in some way such as intuition, a small voice, or just what you notice.

By asking open questions about a subject you will link to the relevant field - but the information obtained may not make sense to you unless you have a good basic knowledge of the subject.

Hence it is best to 'start small' when asking about something, and to then build a good knowledge base which can be expanded.

It seems that Beings such as ArchAngels exist (or operate) in fields - they can exert their influences at many places at the same time.

In this context it seems that Beings such as Arch Angels have specific 'jobs' or skills; asking help from such a Being may not be successful if the job/skill of that Being differs from that requested. Deities seem to be concerned primarily with religious belief systems - they may not help if the subject is not within their scope of operation.

Perhaps it is best to ask your Heart to direct your request to the correct Being, or to ask the 'Good God System' for help, knowing that will link to the correct source of help.

Other sources of fields are the higher levels of souls not now in the physical plane. There have been many examples of people linking to the fields of famous musicians and artists and gaining some of their attributes.

Fields can influence the world of matter. Many chemists have gone through processes which they believe will result in a new formulation having particular properties without success - even when their logic indicates that success should occur.

Suddenly, when a large number of such formulations have occurred, it seems that a field forms which now accepts the formulation and enables it to be successfully repeated.

Other examples of fields include healing modalities such as Reiki, martial arts like Kung Fu, and the most powerful of all, True Holy Love - which is embodied in Namaste. We can link to the field of ME, and when we use that field with True Holy Love all is possible.

The metaphysical world is a world of thought; thus there are fields for characters that have existed only in ones imagination, like comic characters such as Superman - we can link to those characters and so obtain their abilities.

When we imagine something, our mind will access our sub-conscious memories to find whatever resonates most with that imagination.

If the something is not within our own memory, it is easier for our Heart-Mind-Brain team to access the actual situation than to make up a new (and possibly wrong) imaginary image. Thus if we are imagining an actual situation with a person, the true situation will be presented - it resonates best.

Unfortunately this is not always so - if we have a vested interest in the situation then our mind is not fully open, and what we perceive may be what we want, not 'what is'. This helps to explain why we are often more successful in helping others than working miracles on ourselves, family members, and friends.

Working with Morphic Fields

The Morphic Field is a very simple technique to understand. It's also a very easy toy to play with because it is applied like the intent you would apply in any 2-Point process.

In simpler terms, morphic resonance is the process that allows the information contained in morphic fields to act upon an individual or an item.

Matrix Energeticists (MEs) can tap into these morphic fields and use the information in them to effect change with our clients or ourselves. The MEs can focus the morphic resonance of a particular morphic field or fields on whatever subject the practitioner chooses.

I use Morphic Fields to settle things down after a rough session or to bring about a quick, simple change before or during a session.

For example, I was on an airplane recently and another passenger was sneezing and blowing her nose for about half an hour. I could see her about three rows ahead of me, lying down on the seats in the middle section. I asked (God, Higher Power, Universe, etc. -- my personal choice and belief) if it was safe for both of us for me to change her situation. I got YES, so I applied the morphic field of Sudafed. Within seconds the sneezing stopped. Ah . . . peace and quiet !

Here's another example. After a particularly rough session, one of my clients was feeling jittery and mildly frightened and refused to leave the therapy room.

I applied the morphic field of a deprivation tank (watch the movie Daredevil to see one in action). Instantly, she jumped a little and gradually she calmed down. She walked out of the room with no problem.

My favorite feature of Morphic Field is not needing to know how the information in the field works. I've never seen a deprivation tank except in the movie, let alone lay in one. I just figured if I could put her in a place with no stimulus at all, she might calm down.

Obviously, the more you know about the information in the Morphic Field, the better, but it's so cool that you can use it just as effectively if you do almost nothing at all.

Another really useful feature is that you may also use only part of a morphic field instead of everything in it. Let's take Chiropractic Therapy, for example. I don't focus on any specific discipline within it, I simply focus on basic adjustment of the spinal vertebrae. I apply the morphic field and have it continually adjust until all the vertebra are adjusted and then I ask all the adjusted structures to align.

Let's look at Massage Therapy, for another example. Now, since my wife is (no offense to all of you LMTs out there!) the best massage therapist in the whole, wide world, I will use the Morphic Field she has built up throughout her practice. I don't have to have all of Massage Therapy since the beginning of time bombarding my client's body. Instead, I can selectively apply a very specific part of that large morphic field.

So in summation, Morphic Field is a great toy for cleaning up after a session or applying a quick fix. As an extra added bonus, you don't have to know much about the field itself to use it ! Also, remember that you may use a very specific part of the field.

Pre-Session Quick Fix

A woman came in complaining of a headache she'd had for three days.

I figured she had more going on if the headache lasted that long. So, I wanted to spend as little time as I could on the headache.

I asked her what she normally takes for a headache and she said she doesn't like to take anything.

OK, so if you did take something, what would it be ? She said Tylenol. I envisioned a little cloud over her head. This cloud represents the morphic field for Tylenol. I then imagined a ray going from the cloud to her head. The ray represents the morphic resonance. After 30 seconds or so, I asked her how her headache was. "It's less, but I can still feel it". I switched the morphic field from Tylenol to Tylenol Extra Strength. After another 10 seconds or so, she said it seemed to be getting worse. Two seconds after that, she exclaimed, "Oh . . . wait, oh, it's gone!"

The morphic field for allopathic medicine is very strong since many people all over the world use it. Don't be afraid to employ the Morphic Field of medication, like I did with the Sudafed incident I described earlier. Even if your client has physical or emotional reasons for refusing certain or all allopathic medications. Your client will receive all of the benefits of the medicine without any of the side-effects.

<u>In-Session On-going Fix</u>

A woman came complaining of exhaustion. Everyone in her life seemed to be driving her crazy (which usually indicates that it's not everyone else, just you).

I began by Time Traveling back until I found a day (about three weeks earlier) that the stress didn't exist. I envisioned the Archetype (see Chapter 8) of a door marked with the date I just found and together, we went in. As I started to overlay the patterning from that day, she started holding her face and complaining of increasing sinus pressure. I didn't want to stop, so I envisioned three separate Morphic Fields -- Neti Pot, Craniosacral Technique (specifically for the skull) and Accupressure (specifically for the sinuses).

I activated the Morphic Resonance for each and focused them on her head. I left all of them running for as long as they were needed and I returned to the Time Travel.

Once we got her into and stable in the 'No Stress' day, we Time Travelled back to the present, using the big red PRESENT button on my control panel. When I asked her how she felt, she said she felt a lot calmer and she could breathe clearly.

Morphic Fields can be used simultaneously without interfering with each other. In addition, they can be left running in the background while you focus on the more active portions of your play.

Post-Session Integrating Fix

A woman who has liver cancer came in because she wasn't responding well to her treatments.

We determined that her subconscious had a very strong aversion to living life. Once we moved her to a place where she could view living life in a positive manner, she was very unstable -- nauseous, dizzy, tired, nervous, etc. I used a few Archetypes to center, ground and balance her energy.

That made her more stable, but when she got up, she couldn't stand up straight ! Instead, she was bent over at the waist at about a 75-degree angle. We walked out to the reception area, where her sister was sitting on the couch. I used a combination of Morphic Fields -- Cranial Sacral Technique, Feldenkreis Therapy, Alexander Technique, Massage Therapy, Chiropractic Therapy. After letting the fields run for awhile, her sister exclaimed, "Wow! I've never seen you stand up so straight ! You're always so hunched over."

Again, Morphic Fields can be used with very little knowledge of the subject matter within the morphic field. I have never taken a course or had a treatment with most of the therapies above but I have an idea of what they are supposed to do.

All I really need to know is that the Alexander Technique has to do with correcting and maintaining good posture. That seems helpful and so I'll apply it. Feldenkreis Therapy is a movement therapy and I figured if she was less stiff, that may help her to more easily stand up straight.

Morphic Field is one of the simplest toys to play with in the ME toy box, but it is extremely useful in bringing about change in the background. Just like those As Seen On TV ovens, just set it and forget it !

I like to find the morphic field and 2-Point them to it - in this case the morphic field of Traditional Chinese Medicine and then go to the subset of herbal medicine and 2-Point it to wherever it wants to go. I did this with a guy who had neck pain for 10 years and tried all kinds of modalities. I accessed the morphic field of acupuncture and 2-Pointed him to it. His pain went away.

Thought Forms

Everything that exists has been formed by thought. When we make something, we first think about what we are going to make, usually based on forming different patterns from other things that presently exist - such as mixing flour, yeast, and water to make bread.

We learn how to do this from others - watching them or reading their instructions. The process works because it has been done before - it has a field of information.

Leadbeater and Besant wrote a book 'Thought Forms' which includes coloured pictures of the forms developed by different types of music, which they could see clairvoyantly. They also show the shapes and colours of thought forms of anger and hate seen in a person's aura.

Dr Emoto in his book 'Message from Water' shows pictures of the water crystals formed by various thoughts. Those formed with love are beautiful; the ones where the water was labelled with hate and anger look ghastly.

It is interesting to see that the crystals formed from homeopathic remedies showed miniature pictures of the plants used - is this an example of the holographic form of the universe? We can recognize that the field of the plant has been incorporated into the water crystal - it 'morphed' the water with the essence of the plant's own field.

When we examine the non-physical planes we find that they consist completely of thought - in fields and in forms. Those that have form seem, in many cases, to exert fields that influence thought.

Chapter 8

Create a way that is new, so Angelic Beings find it fun to do !

Archetypes

All in this chapter was written by a Matrix Energeticist.

The Archetype is the most versatile and possibly the most exciting tool in your ME toolbox. It can vary from a simple two-dimensional shape to the Starship Enterprise. You are literally limited only by your imagination. The more wild and creative you get with your archetype, the more effective it will be! So what is an archetype, anyway? In psychological terms, an archetype is an original pattern that subsequent representations are modeled after.

In ME, an archetype is sort of the opposite. The ME archetype is a representation that replaces an existing system or structure - creating a new framework, which allows a simpler approach to an existing situation

Archetypes can replace complicated systems with simple representations, like a large cloth for a headache.

Archetypes can create an object to trigger an effect, like using a sump pump to drain excess fluid in a body.

Archetypes allow you to create physiological changes without any need to understand the mechanism(s) required for that change.

Archetypes also give your logical mind something that makes sense so it can play along!

Archetypes give you the freedom to release an army of PacMen to gobble up a disease instead of struggling and fighting it. So let's feast instead of fight! It's a lot easier and a lot more fun!!

OK, let's walk through that one again, but a whole lot slower. It might be easier to illustrate this concept with a few stories.

Headache

A woman came with a litany of complaints that ended with, "and on top of all that, I have a headache, too!!".

As soon as she said that I pictured in my mind's eye a table with all sorts of stuff on it, completely covered with a large white cloth. I 2-Pointed her temples and then grasped the ends of the large cloth and yanked it off. The table was still there with all the stuff on top of it but the large cloth was gone. I asked her how her headache was right now. She blinked, frowned and said, "That's weird but it feels like it's gone."

Work with whatever image comes to you. Notice what you notice! Because I saw the cloth-covered table and she mentioned that her headache was on top of all the other problems she had, it made sense to remove whatever was on top of everything else.

Edema

A woman came in complaining of swelling in her lower leg. Did the press test and she had a mild case of edema with normal skin temperature. The normal skin temperature indicated that it wasn't a lymphatic swelling due to some kind of injury. She said it just popped up one day and never went away.

Edema is a circulatory problem where fluid collects in bodily tissues or cavities where very little or no fluid is normally present. Armed with this *medical knowledge,* I knew exactly what I needed to do!

First, I would need to stop the flow of anymore fluid into the tissues.

Second, I would need to dry up the existing excess fluid.

Simple! I envisioned a faucet handle on each knee and promptly turned them off. Then I put a space heater in each calf to dry up the excess fluid.

She looked uncomfortable, so I asked her how she was feeling. She said that her legs felt tighter and hot now. *Now that wasn't supposed to happen!!* I undid everything immediately and the new symptoms began reversing.

So instead of focusing on the excess fluid, I turned my focus to her circulation. I put a sump pump in each foot and asked her how she felt right now. She said she felt a little weird because her legs and pelvic area were all tingly like when a foot falls asleep and starts waking up again. Over about a 20 minute period, the intensity of the tingling decreased to nothing. Her left lower leg showed no signs of edema but her right lower leg was still a bit swollen.

I moved her to a place (parallel universe) where her whole body had no blockages. She felt an instantaneous pinch of pain in her lower back that faded almost immediately. She slowly leaned back and closed her eyes and stayed that way for about 10 minutes. When she came out of it, both legs showed no signs of edema and the dull headache she had (but didn't mention) was gone.

Focus on the cause and not the symptoms: Dr Bartlett always advised to ignore the warning of the great and powerful Oz.

DO look at the little man behind the curtain because that's where your solution is. Dealing with symptoms, often times, won't get you anything but frustrated. When I focused on eliminating the excess fluid in her tissues (aka the symptom) it made everything worse by creating new symptoms. By focusing on her circulation (aka the cause) and pumping out all of the excess fluid in her tissues her edema subsided.

Poor Hearing

A girl came in with her mother. The mother was complaining that her daughter's iPod was so loud it was driving her crazy. The girl was wearing her iPod with her earbuds in. I was standing about five feet away and I could hear her music pretty clearly.

Had her take her earbuds out. First I tuned her ears by rotating them, one at a time, like a dial on an analog radio. I turned her ears until they were tuned into a station that she really liked. After that I had her try her iPod again.

She cringed from sound and turned the volume down. She could hear a lot better in her right ear and it was better in the left ear, too - but it was still a bit soft. So next, I pulled her left ear away from her head like a television's rabbit ear, looking for better reception. First a foot, then 5 feet, 10 feet, and so on and so on. After pulling it away from her head 760 feet and angling it around a bit, she said her ear popped. She put her iPod in and had to turn the volume down a bit more. Her hearing was fine now, in both ears.

Use your own experience for inspiration. When I heard what the mother was saying, it just popped into my head that she was just not getting good reception. I'm old enough ... very experienced with slowly turning the tuning dial on car radios to get rid of picket-fencing and fiddling with rabbit ears for hours trying to get better reception. By using techniques I am very familiar with and have been very successful with, I greatly increased my odds for success.

Fatigue

A woman came in saying that she was feeling run down all week. Nothing was really going on but she wasn't sleeping well and figured that's why she was so tired. Just to let you know, lack of sleep is usually never the cause, it's an effect. I asked her if she was sure nothing else was going on and nothing out of the ordinary was going on. Then I asked her if there was anything coming up.

She did have her husband's, cousin's daughter's wedding to go to next Saturday. She mumbled that was going to be stuck with her in-laws, but since it was only for two days, she was fine about it.

Since she came in all run down, I figured I would do like Hanz und Franz from Saturday Night Live and PUMP HER UP! After establishing a 2-Point, instead of weights, I used an archetype of a home aquarium fish pump. I plugged the hose into the middle of her back and let it run. After a minute or two, she said she wasn't feeling as tired.

Since she was mired down in the thoughts about the wedding, I saw her feelings of dread and despair as and archetype of a large swamp with her stuck in the middle. I plucked her little image from the center of the swamp and moved it to another archetype of a quiet, white sand beach. I asked her to imagine this same deserted beach and told her that as long as her in-laws were around, she could stay here on this beach. She half-slumped into her lap. When she came back up she was feeling a lot more relaxed, clear-minded and, in her words, "Soooooo caaaaalllmmmm."

Use your client's body language. For example, observing that she was dragging when she walked in, inspired me to use the fish pump, "pump her up."

Use your client's words and tone of voice. By saying that she was going to be stuck with her in-laws with such a depressed, defeated tone of voice, that conjured up an image for me of her trapped in a dark, stinky swamp. The beautiful, deserted beach seemed like the greatest contrast. All these archetypes allowed both of us to reframe her entire experience.

[JML: There were quite a few comments about seeing Angels, and how Angels told that they were bored ! It seems that using an Archetype gives the ME Beings/ Angels more fun, since they have a puzzle to solve.]

Letting go

Letting go simply means allowing your intention to be free.

For example, I had a woman who came in saying that she couldn't raise her arm higher than this (parallel to the floor). Let's use that to illustrate the template above:

Step 1: I established a 2-Point by holding her wrist and touching a point where her neck meets her shoulder.

Step 2: I pictured in my mind's eye, the woman raising her hand like an enthusiastic child in school.

Step 3: I said, "Go!"

During Step 3, I mentally send the picture out into the universe. Just imagine holding a photograph in your hand and tossing it out like a Frisbee and watching it's molecules disperse into space.

Or just imagine the photograph becomes a pebble in your hand and you toss it in a pond, watching the ripples travel the breadth of the pond. Create your own method, that makes sense to you. Creating a method that makes sense to you, IS THE KEY to letting go.

So what about the lady with the arm?

Oh right! So anyway, the woman's head dropped down and her arm swirled round-and-round in slow circles. In my mind's eye I could see the circles kept getting larger and larger and suddenly, her head just dropped. I removed my hands and she slowly raised her head and sleepily opened her eyes. I asked her how her arm felt and she slowly raised it to the point where the pain was supposed to kick in and it didn't. Soon she had a big smile on her face and was flapping her arm like a one-winged bird.

I've had clients feel pain, nausea, headaches during and after their sessions. I've had clients get stuck to the wall or the table and even throw up during sessions. Does that mean ME is doing harm? ABSOLUTELY NOT!

The night after my first Level 1 seminar, I was practicing with one of my seminar-mates. She listed a litany of personal problems and issues that she wanted to have cleared. In retrospect, I should have addressed them one-by-one but instead, I did one 2-Point and asked the question, "What would it feel like if I was free of all of my conflicts?" The next 90 minutes was filled with everything from crying and wailing to animal imitations. It was a really wild ride!!

After all that was over, she was tired but her body felt lighter and her head felt clearer.

HOORAY!! The next day, she was waiting in the hotel lobby for me. She felt nauseous, had a headache and was having a hard time breathing. NOT HOORAY!!

She had gone to see Dr Bartlett and was quite irritated with his response, because he said, "Great! You're experiencing all kind of changes!!" I was able to clear most of it before I went to class that morning.

So did I cause harm because I was conflicted? No, I didn't. Even though she was suffering, Dr Bartlett saw her changes as positive. The changes that we created in her were positive for her, but her body, mind, spirit and soul needed to adjust to all of the emotional and physiological changes. She just needed time to process and integrate all of the changes. In my experience, the whole process and integration takes about 48 hours.

So what do you do if your clients call and say they can't stand how they're feeling the next morning? Don't circumvent their evolution - assist it instead!

Simply 2-Point them remotely and put them in a place where the processing is 10 times faster, or maybe is already done.

You could set an intention to do no harm, but I wouldn't. What you consider harm might be exactly what your client needs to release whatever ails them. It might be better to take a more positive approach and set an intention to allow me the freedom to do only the greatest good for myself and my client.

Remember that seminar-mate I made feel so terrible? I never heard from her again but she did refer a friend of hers to me about six months later. So the transition away from the negative can be painful, but it is a transition toward the positive.

More Hints

First and foremost, can you feel how much energy you are investing in successfully not succeeding? I would 2-Point you to a place where you understand that you have not failed losing weight the last of times, but that you have found of ways NOT to lose weight.

If you see yourself as someone on a continuing journey instead of someone who's at a dead end after dead end. This will help you feel motivated instead of deflated. Be the Shining Star you are.

Secondly, 2-Point your insight and have it scour you to find out what the payoff is for keeping the weight on.

Remember two things:

1) The Secret: Everything you believe will come true.

2) Your subconscious (emotional) mind, where your beliefs reside, has one main job -- to protect you.

If a part or parts of you believe that your extra weight is necessary to keep you safe in your life, for whatever reason, then you'll never lose a single ounce. It would be like a knight throwing off all of his armor and going into battle.

Last, but certainly not least, love you (ALL OF YOU) as you would everyone and everything you care about. 2-Point you to a place where your heart space is extended to include you, again, every part of your mind, body, spirit and soul. The more you don't like that part of you, the more you need to include it.

To that end, 2-Point yourself to three places in the following order and in succession upon completion of each level:

1) Be completely and thoroughly grateful to you for all you have brought to you -- everything.

2) Understand you completely and thoroughly: why you say what you say, why you do what you do, why you are the way you are, why you are who you are.

3) Forgive you completely and thoroughly for everything: everything you have ever said, everything you have ever done, everything you have been, are and will be.

Once you've passed these three levels, everything I offered earlier will be much easier. After that, CELEBRATE YOU!!

When in your heart space you have access to the field of possibilities. You don't do anything - you ALLOW the field to bring to you (like a dog bringing you your slippers) what is needed in that moment in space/time.

Playing with my client today I was attracted to her thyroid, which brought me to her nervous system which brought in an archetype - it's just a flow of information, showing up as a thyroid or archetype. Sometimes I pause till the next bit of information is brought in to my heart space and then my right brain shows me what it is with symbolism.

Through the whole session of 45 minutes I never left my Heart Space; I TRUST that the information needed will show up and then I ALLOW. This keeps me in the state of PLAYFUL JOY (oneness with the all) and not having a left-brain belief that I am separate and must do something external to myself to bring about a change.

When not getting along with somebody I take both me and the other person to another reality where we are getting along great - maybe sitting in a virtual hot tub laughing and joking and having a great time. Just having fun with any matrix tool.

Notes:

> The Angelic Beings, like most people, get bored doing 'the same old thing' all of the time. Use your imagination to form a new method, making it FUN - and it will be done!

Chapter 9 *The Frequencies we call from Above Are Angelic Beings working with Love*

Colours and Frequencies

Each colour that we see has a specific frequency in the physical plane, within the octave of our visual range. There are colours in the octaves above and below our human visual range, some of which are seen by other animals, in the same way that they can hear sounds above or below our range of hearing.

Each element has its own 'bars' of colour, which are used by scientists to determine the composition of materials and of distant stars and planets - allowing for the shift due to movement, the basis of Radar, similar to the way that the siren of an ambulance (or police vehicle) is heard differently if it is approaching us or going away.

Each colour has its own characteristics; perhaps it is also the case that every healing thought has its own 'bars' of colours, similar to a mix of elements in a material.

TouchStones

On the back cover of this book are pictures of 21 'TouchStones', as sometimes used by US astronauts when travelling in space to maintain good health. The actual TouchStones are no longer available, but I believe that their energy is incorporated into the pictures - linked to an actual set that I possess.

The pictures on the back cover are reproductions of those illustrated in the 'Distant Healing Manual' that I wrote, and which is a free download from my website www.in2it.ca - at the end of the 'Healing Overview' section.

In that manual I explain how to use a Pendulum to locate where colour healing is needed in a person's body, organs, and aura; how to determine which colour is needed; and how to load that colour for healing.

Dr Bartlett has been given 21 Frequencies for healing - perhaps some of them are the same. Note that these are really Vibrational Patterns that operate in the frequencies of a medium such as sound, light, thought, etc.

He has also discovered that the frequencies can be inverted, to give different effects - similar to the way that Radionic healing identifies the frequencies causing a problem, and then sends the inverse to nullify the causes.

Richard Bartlett suggests that you imagine that you have a slide-bar that goes from OFF to FULL for each frequency, and that you raise each one in turn to become acquainted with it and its effects.

I have worked at feeling the effect of Dr Bartlett's frequencies in the way that he suggests. I have heard 'clicks' that indicate that they have been doing healing on myself, but I have not yet succeeded in visualizing their colours or having any major feeling of them or their actions. I trust that you will be more successful !

I did the above while sitting down. Later, when standing up, I asked to feel the effect of each frequency, and my body swayed making patterns - the 'wave' that is mentioned so often by Matrix Energeticists.

A great many Matrix Energeticists are enthusiastic about these frequencies, and use them with wonderful healing results.

Note that the numbers given are labels or names, not the actual electro-magnetic frequency.

Frequencies

Frequency Zero - F0 - is the Eternal Portal. Both giving and receiving; endlessly, simultaneously. Yet it neither gives nor receives by it's own device. It does not limit nor choose nor define. Neither negative nor positive, it does not contain.

Frequency One - F1 - *Color:* Red-gold

Attributes: This frequency enhances the energy of the body and vitalizes the body as a whole. It brings information into cellular structures; streamlines the flow of information in the energetic matrix; and also brings energy and enthusiasm to your thoughts, emotions, or situations. F1 is warm or hot and often intense in nature.

It adds vitality - F1 can sometimes add vitality to symptoms i.e. make them worse. Try inverting the frequency to calm symptoms. (I do this when I get a burn while cooking. The result is no blister or pain.)

F1 inverted: Invert it to take energy/vitality out of old patterns and conditions, such as negative thoughts, allergies, colds. flu, illness, infections, pain conditions, disturbed sleep patterns and even traffic congestions.

Before retiring last night I decided to invert F1 to see what would happen in my sleep and found I slept deeply with many vivid dreams which I was able to recall in the morning.

For me, I like to put F1 into all my meals to stuff them full of energy and ramp up the nutritious value. Today, I'm going to do my best to turn it on and off throughout the day and see what I notice.

I like to put F1 in my shower head so that I can bathe in it, and I have used it in my decaf tea when I want a better jolt like the regular caffeinated tea gives me. Despite the heat wave, I sold a lot of tea today. F1 revitalized my cash register !

After work my hubby and I will be going on a hike in the Sierra Mts to watch the sunset around the Lake Tahoe area, so I will use F1 to be energized for the evening! ! I have also used it before an evening of dancing, and we have friends who perform, and they can really feel the difference when I shower not only them, but the audience with F1. One time I put F1 in the spotlight that shone on a band member who was having a severe medical issue, and for the first time in weeks he walked off the stage rather than having to crawl off after his performance.

I also like adding F1 to my water bottle in the office and showering it over my granddaughter's softball game to make it a little more lively !

Frequency Two - F2 - *Color:* Electric blue or blue-white

Attributes: Electrical in nature, this frequency governs anything having to do with the nervous system and/or the adaptations made because of it. This works through the nervous system and the polarities and dualities of experience. By inverting the frequency, excess energy can be reversed or cancelled out. Inverted, this is useful for insomnia and ADD.

As mentioned above, for clients and myself, I drop F2 often into the body to increase wound healing, balance out meridian's and chakras, help with vision issues.

I have used it with clients who have MS, head injuries and brain transmitter problems (along with some other modules) to help recreate nerve pathways.

I have used F2 to help with courage (more Nerve !) to face ceremonial work or helping to confront in relationship situations. I use it to assist computer problems, and mechanical problems on cars, batteries and cell phone when it needs that little bit more charge to get me thru the day to where I can recharge it.

It has appeared on it's own to assist with heart situations, and I have used it, successfully, to connect on a more electrical basis, the head and heart centers. It is also great with recharging other organ systems, like the pancreas and to increase circulation (of blood, lymph, ideas, and balancing body systems).

I have used F2 along with time lines and 'In Utero' conditions with very dramatic use on helping assist with life long unbalanced feelings of body from left to right. Both the client and myself 'saw' the fetal first cells reorganizing and balancing.

Interestingly, she and I did not describe this 'feeling' as electrical, even though F2 showed up, it felt like a rubber band. Could be the

F2 + F3 Recreation frequencies Richard talks about, although I only recognized the F2 at the time.

I have used F2 Inverted quite often to assist with clients who have nerve pain/damage, like with shingles, PHN conditions, spinal pain. It works great inverted (many cases using it) with bringing down triple warmer meridian for anxiety states. Sometimes I 'paint' the inverted F2 on.

Using F2 inverted also helps with tinnitus (ringing in the ears). Of course it also has helped with sleep. So you run this frequency which is electric blue. Pretty intense. Invert it and you now get a calming energy.

Frequency Three - F3 -*Color:* Rose/pink/scarlet

Attributes: This frequency feels very enveloping and loving, with a magnetic or emanating quality. It is harmonizing and balancing, and it gives a sense of a rotation of energy. Its energy is perpendicular to the energy of frequency two; together they join in a figure-eight relationship, creating electromagnetism.

Harmonize the allergy sufferer with the allergen. Use F3 just for a general feeling of well-being and contentedness. I'm noticing that other people's bad moods aren't affecting me as much. Instead, I find that I'm able to see that their mood is a reflection of their current state and that I don't have to join them in that state.

As a root frequency vibrationally (carrying aspects of 1st chakra), I can see where this frequency is an important aspect to combine with the electrical aspects of F2 and the vitality aspects of F1 to complete the triune of survivability.

"Whew! It saved my sanity this morning. Day 2 of summer holidays and I'm noticing more grey hair. They're climbing walls, screaming, hitting each other, etc. Its too rainy and cold to send them outside. All I did was think of F3 and they have been in their own bedrooms reading books and doing puzzles for the last half hour. It is so peaceful and quiet that I almost forgot that they are home ! Sending every mother on the planet F3, including our Earth Mother."

"When I turned on F3 yesterday, I reread the description in my notes and realized that I had been using it just for magnetic transformation, which works great. It really assists in circulation and lymph flow problems, and such. I use it often, as Richard mentions, along with F2 as an electro-magnetic balance."

Frequency Four - F4 - *Color:* Brown/black

Attributes: This frequency aids in the physical restructuring of muscle, bone, tendons, joints, and fascia. It can be applied to aches and pains like a salve, and it is also grounding. The color may manifest as dark and crystalline, like instant coffee granules.

I spread the brown salve all over lower back and hips....like a mud spa treatment. Know that F4 can solve aches and pains, so request it, wrap it around like a salve and trust all will unfold.

One of the items in the description says that Frequency Four can help restructure finances. I'm paying my bills today and sending Frequency Four into each check I write. F4 increased verbal clarity.

Frequency Five - F5 - *Color:* Rose pink

Attributes: This frequency is a universal love essence, warm and personal like a mother's love. It affects intercellular communication, interacting with all the systems in your body, as well as your activities, thoughts, and feelings.

Inverted F5, takes you out of rapport with the state you are experiencing.

Frequency Six - F6 - *Color:* Clear with highlights of blue and green; also emerald green.

Attributes: This frequency is related to the womb of creation, and it works on issues of ancestral healing as well as our own in-utero patterns and experiences. Comforting and soothing, watery and gel-like in appearance, this frequency is useful for dissolving longstanding emotional and mental traumas. It has been used to heal tumors, which are essentially embryonic tissue.

Wrap F6 around the client when she's feeling needy and clingy.

Frequency Seven - F7 - *Color:* Burnt orange/earth tones

Attributes: This frequency can be thought of as a life-force battery for depleted states. It is both grounding and detoxifying, and it affects the relationship between the physical body and the emotions. Useful for endocrine adaptations to emotion and regulation of hormones, and in transforming cellular memory of deep emotion, particularly fear. Related to kidney chi; warming.

The use of F7 is described as emotion affecting the physical template.

Frequency Eight - F8 - *Color:* Iridescent/mother-of-pearl

Attributes: F8 represents the integration of the previous seven frequencies. On a personal level, it brings integration to experiences, activities, and understanding. Unity, balance, and flow are the keywords. This frequency moves long-term habits, personality, and emotional structures as they relate to soul evolution.

It is great to help us understand information. If we do not understand something we can turn on F8 and lasso it around the subject and F8 will help us grasp it.

Inverted F8 undoes nasty patterns.

Frequency Nine - F9 - *Color:* Translucent

Attributes: Distinctly different from all other frequencies, frequency nine can be thought of as a 'spiritual cleanser'. It cleans the spiritual essence of the body and defrags the spiritual hard drive. This energy is a fast-moving, intense, animated intelligence that clears the body of accumulated energetic interference patterns.

It is used for clearing entities, aberrant mental thought forms, curses, and interpersonal energetic interactions.

Run F9 and reverse it to let in guardian angels to ask them to rid the subject of any lingering entities.

Frequency Ten - F10 - *Color:* Translucent or metallic red

*Attributes:*This frequency is the mirror image of frequency five, representing protective father energy. The warrior aspect of love, it is discriminating and dividing, and its love is like a shield.

A powerful yet surprisingly gentle energy which gives strength and resolve, it permeates the aura, physical body, emotions, and mental body.

I use F10 as a big spherical shield offering protection inside and guiding trouble makers to a new path.

Frequency Eleven - F11 - *Color:* Woodland green

Attributes: Mothering and nurturing, like a tropical rain forest, this frequency is the antidote to living in a concrete jungle. It has the energy of a nurturing earth mother, and it helps drop blood pressure, regulate heart beat, and bring warmth to the body.

Frequency Twelve - F12 - *Color:* Oily black

Attributes: This frequency governs the repair of the body's energy centers, swirling into these vortexes to cleanse the chakras and remove debris from energetic patterns. It often appears as a thick, viscous fluid.

Frequency Thirteen - F13 - *Color:* Crystalline, like quartz

Attributes: Crystalline in color and feel, this frequency is a component of the DNA morphogenetic field surrounding organisms and species, with the DNA serving as the antennae that patterns information from the field into physical expression.

This energy interfaces with a template just beyond the physical and restructures the fields that influence our genetic template.

Frequency Fourteen - F14 - *Color:* Obsidian black, moss green

Attributes: This cooling, soothing frequency is almost homeopathic in its effect, detoxifying the energy field and changing the vibrations of the physical cellular template. It works on the 'basement' of the cellular matrix, evoking change from the bottom up.

<u>Frequency Fifteen</u> - F15 - *Color:* Vibrant emerald or teal

Attributes: This frequency governs the flow of information through hormonal and circulatory systems, and it rearranges the magnetic, electrical, and biochemical strategies of the body. Interfacing with circulation, the endocrine system, and cellular communication; F15 clears the physical circuitry and can be very useful for balancing hormones and the states they produce.

<u>Frequency Sixteen</u> - F16 - *Color:* No color - **Ocean shades of gray, blue, or green.**

Attributes: This is the frequency of unconditional love. When it manifests, it often involves the experience of dolphins and whales. It sometimes carries ocean shades of gray, blue, and green. This frequency is joyful, playful, nonjudgmental, relaxing, calming, and grounding. It is useful for clearing inappropriate emotions and for working with emotional states, including depression and loss. Comforting, loving, and funny, it brings new perspectives and awareness.

<u>Frequency Seventeen</u> - F17 - *Color:* Golden, grid-like

Attributes: This frequency is used in the functional physiology, anatomical, and the biochemical processes of the body.

It affects systemic processes of the body, and it appears as self-intelligent lattices of interlocking grids. This frequency moves the Assemblage Beam. It may appear as self-intelligent golden interlocking grids.

<u>Frequency Eighteen</u> - F18 - *Color:* Red-brown

Attributes: This frequency can awaken involuntary yoga or T'ai Chi types of movements and contortions. It is linked to trance states, the rising of the kundalini, and crown chakra expansion.

This pre-physical, primordial consciousness induces involuntary motions and recalibrates the physical body. Frequency eighteen often interacts with F17.

Frequency Nineteen - F19 - *Color:* Luminescent gold or yellow

Attributes: Nineteen is useful for reigniting the divine spark and accessing soul communion. It brings profound inner rest and stillness, and it allows you to experience deep meditative states without the practice of meditation. It allows you to experience the unified field, inverts pathological patterns of information, and re-establishes divinity within patterns of disease.

Frequency Twenty - F20 - *Color:* Quartz white

Attributes: Crystalline in nature, this frequency contains quantum states of information.

It cleanses chakras, meridians, spaces, and emotions, and it heals the crystal matrices of the body, reconnecting the heart and mind. It can instantly transform so-called negative vibrations. Programmable, with an independent intelligence, it may also be able to magnify other frequencies.

Frequency Twenty-One - F21 - *Color:* White

Attributes: Useful in exploring inner space, this frequency can bring instantaneous journeys, including lucid dreaming and travel to shamanic worlds. It is associated with multidimensional layers of consciousness, parallel universes, soul retrieval, and space/time travel. This frequency is helpful for retrieving information from the field and for communing with spirit entities.

Frequency 22 - F22 -'who cares', 'whatever' kind of frequency....it has same qualities as let go, or get out of the way but it works for me when I can't let go because this way it is 'doing nothing' wrapped in 'doing' kind of package.

It supercharges one's ability to let go of things. When you turn it up, it almost like you can sense the burden that you are carrying (on your shoulder, etc) and help you to energetically let go of the burden.

It gives you the sensation of throwing the unwanted emotions (fear, anxiety, etc) to the sea knowing that letting go is the essence of constructing a new and productive reality.

Once you let go, your shoulder would feel lighter than before. When you let go, trust that a new and better reality will show up in the next moment.

You can use this frequency after 2 pointing or after another frequency as it can help you to improve your result.

Frequency 27 - F27 - Co-ordinates Frequencies, assigning them as needed

Frequency 32 - F32 - heaven on earth, and a burst of rainbow colors

Frequency 257 - F257 - the frequency of UNLIMITED KNOWLEDGE. Drop down to your heart and ask for this frequency to come to you.

Using Frequencies

Here are some fun ideas:

Day Care - Bring in F5 (unconditional Love) with F10 (protective love) and F16 for fun and learning.

Electrician try F2 and F3, but in a friendly way so you don't become the live wire.

Heating and air conditioning - use F1 for heating, inverted F1 for cooling breezes.

Spiritual retreat center - F19 and F21

Dive Shop - just F16

Dentist - F9 to clear out all the bad mojo everyone has around going to the dentist.

Garden Center F1, F11 and F14 for growing green everywhere.

Computer Shop F2 and F3 in filter mode so folks don't blow the circuits.

Lingerie store F15 for hormones and frequency 69 for... wait whoops wrong topic.

To bring in business roll F1 and F5 out like a red carpet to welcome people in. Turn F2 and F3 on to 'electrify' the environment and get people excited.

In other words ask yourself what frequency would be useful and plug your mixing board cord into source then crank the volume. Give an imaginary Eddie Van Halen a guitar and amp tuned to that frequency and let him rock the house.

Let it come out your eyes if you like, or maybe your finger tips and then spray paint it all over the place.

I am a chiropractor so I use a lot of F1-F4 but when I have been treating more complicated cases the universe has a sense of humor and a great way to keep you humble.

When I have a string of great outcomes the universe sends someone to me that terrifies my left brain so I use a question, "If I knew what to do what would that be?"

The answer in this case was to bring in F14 from the sacrum, since it evokes changes from the bottom up, I visualize it as a black/green vortex spinning clockwise. Simultaneously I bring in F17 from above the head spinning counterclockwise going down through the body.

The results in this case were the disappearance of knee pain 'caused' by degenerative joint disease and no longer needing antidepressants.

Opening an inverted frequency does the opposite of the regular frequency. So if F1 increases energy and vitality, then inverting F1 depletes energy and vitality of the surroundings. Keep in mind these only operate if useful.

For example I have used inverted F1 when in situations with others where uncontrolled energy was an issue (e.g. when people were arguing heatedly; when we were on a train with highly drunk out-of-control soccer fans). You could envision inverted F1 also being helpful in removing energy from a spreading infection or cancer. Each of the frequencies can be inverted when/if that is useful.

Just got back from South America and thought I'd share some ME fun and maybe some learning experiences.

-- First off for those of you worried about the new porno-scanners, none of them seemed to be in working condition during my travels. I had 2-Pointed the magic smoke out of them previous to traveling.

-- All my luggage always arrives when and where it's supposed too. I 2-Pointed it to make it easily both directions.

-- Airline agents, customs, TSA, and immigration agents are all very helpful when you broadcast Reiki along with F5. It is amazing how much people perk right up without knowing why.

-- F10 is a great way to wrap yourself and you family if you are at all concerned about crime.

I had one incident where would be thieves closed on my wife's camera, they decided to change venues abruptly as the energy changed. (OK maybe it helps that I look a little scary, but F10 is definitely part of my system since I'd prefer not to have to cause destruction).

-- The only illness encountered was a little bit of altitude sickness brought on by not watching our hydration (it's kind of a combo thing). It cleared up quickly.

-- Had a mix-up with tickets in Miami, 2-Pointed the path to the person who could help and beamed F5 in all directions, the seas (of people) parted and allowed me to get the help needed with no waiting.

-- Had a Hotel mix-up and was able to adjust reality for a timely solution.

A couple of things I've noticed though where improvements will happen:

-- I have rooms at home imprinted with Matrix, Reiki and other beneficial energies so that sometimes I don't even need to intend, it just happens as I focus on the situation. I will be changing it so that these energies are also always in my personal bubble at the same intensity or more.

-- Be careful about asking for the opportunity to adjust reality, suddenly like a hurdler you will create numerous chances to overcome situations.

I adore the frequencies and use them all the time. They are my companions and friends.

They are a system of healing and transformation all unto themselves as they are self intelligent. Each seminar I go to, it seems more uses are given for different ones - especially the level 1 seminars... F1 straight up to enliven and energize and reverse to take the aliveness out of pain, etc.

I use F5 inverted a lot to take me out of rapport with uncomfortable energies I am feeling. You can develop your own relationship with the frequencies and they can teach you, if you are paying attention. I also love it when the higher numbered frequencies come in for a person or situation ... F34, 51, 71, 103, etc.

I use inverted frequencies often when they show up.

The two most stark examples I will never forget involved inverting frequency 1 in threatening situations. So instead of energizing a situation, it drained the energy completely out of the situation (for whatever was useful - keep in mind these are self intelligent). ie F8, undoes nasty patterns, F5, takes you out of rapport with the state you are experiencing.

I'm notorious for running my cell phone out of battery power, so it occurred to me to run F2 & F3 into the battery to charge it up.

I've now done this so many times I've dubbed it the Palm Charger.

So just to really bend what you think is real, I just had one of my children ask me to charge batteries for her remote. Putting them on the palm charger and checking my window to see when they were done I charged them up using F2 & F3 the same way. They weren't even re-chargeable batteries !

At the Taj Mahal my friend's camera run out of batteries. Another friend just basically 2-Pointed it, not knowing anything about frequencies - I had just told him a few words about ME a couple of days before. They could take 127 more pictures.

A client going through painful breakup and stressful housing transition started to have a panic attack on the table ... immediately F5 came in to alleviate ... took about 5 minutes then she was totally clear.

An obnoxious person came to work with intent to cause harm ... again F5 showed up, along with F6, F7, F9, F10. The situation diffused and the person left.

I use F1, F2, and F3 together to 'recharge' people. F3 is handy for balancing out folks who are 'amped' or jittery.

If the frequencies haven't show up as inverted when working they haven't needed to be inverted. Remember that they are self intelligent - so they may have inverted themselves without you being aware of it. It is very rare that they show up that way for me, but I have a meta-rule that allows them to do stuff without me even knowing what they are doing.

Notes:

The key is the Vibrational Pattern - which operates in all mediums according to the frequency of that medium - such as sound, light, and thought.

Chapter 10 *Vibrational Pattern form 'All that Is' Radionics alters them like a Kiss*

Radionics

Everything that exists has a vibrational pattern; this pattern can exist in many forms - in sound, in the electro-magnetic spectrum, as light waves, as thought, and be in morphic fields. It is the actual vibrational pattern, and the energies associated with that pattern, that are important.

In normal Radionics a container has the pattern to be defined, there are dials to register numbers, and a 'sticky pad' on which the operator rubs a finger to determine which number on each dial is correct.

Books have been compiled to list the corrective numbers that should be used to overcome/correct the identified problematic patterns that have been determined.

The corrective numbers are entered on the dials, and a token (such as a photograph, a blood sample, or a hair) of the person to be healed is placed in the outlet. The Radionics machine is then switched on to send the corrective vibrational pattern to the intended person.

The first machines were made of physical parts, and were accepted by the medical community. Later it was found (and publicized) that the machine worked even when the batteries were missing ! This moved it from the medical acceptable list to the non-acceptable list - it was now too 'weird' for those embedded in the physical world to accept. But it still worked!

How can this be?

Getting Numbers

First let us look at the most critical part of the Radionics machine - where decisions are made. The operator rubs his finger on a 'sticky pad', where his finger sticks when the dial number is correct.

How do the fingers know when to stick - even when the token is a photographic print that has never been touched by the person being treated?

Somehow a connection has been made between the operator and the person being treated; perhaps it is a connection between their Hearts and/or minds.

I understand that a person's Heart-Mind-Brain team, working with the 'Wisdom of the Being', knows everything about the person. I know that my Heart can (and does) connect to the Heart of those on whom I work.

I perceive that when I ask for the information that is needed to help another person to heal, my Heart so connects and obtains the needed information.

This is then relayed to me using Dowsing techniques, such as a 'sticky pad' - by my Heart-Mind-Brain team manipulating my nervous-muscular system to give a signal.

How were the books compiled to list the corrective numbers? Possibly by experience; but even then the compilers had to find those numbers - and I suggest that they were found in exactly the same way as the numbers which identify the problems.

I can certainly ask my Heart for what is needed to help someone to heal - and go further, and ask my Heart to send it.

Paper Doctor & Sai Sanjeevini Cards

Some years ago a book called 'The Paper Doctor' was written, that had loads of symbols that cured various diseases.

This was perceived as a threat to the profits of the pharmaceutical companies, so they organized their vassal, the American Medical Association, to get a court order to prevent sales of the book. I actually have a copy of the 'The Paper Doctor'.

The domain of the American Medical Association is restricted to the USA, in the same way that the Canadian Medical Association is confined to Canada. Thus they have not been able to stop the Sai Sanjeevini radionic cards that were developed in India for the poor and others who lacked access to a doctor.

There are about 70 cards for body parts, and about 200 for various diseases - including those which western medicine considers incurable, such as Parkinson's disease, multiple sclerosis, and even AIDS.

All that you have to do is determine the disease, etc. either by being told by a doctor (who may not be correct) or by Dowsing - run your finger down the list of cards until it sticks, or use your Pendulum to point to the needed card. More than one card can be used.

Then you can use various ways to send the corrective vibrational pattern to the person that needs the treatment; one way is to place a glass of water over the cards for at least 15 seconds while 'praying' or using your Pendulum to load the vibrational patterns of the cards into the water - which then becomes medicine.

Now since these cards have been used successfully for many years, they have their own morphic fields. So there may be an even simpler way of doing this healing work.

If I am getting all this information through my Heart, and my Heart is also involved in getting the healing sent where needed, why should I personally be adding so much detail - which is of no real use to me?

Can we not rely on our Heart to link with the Heart of the needy person, with instructions to identify what is wrong, find out what correction is needed, and implement all the work that is needed?

Keyboarding - Organic Radionics

When I was attending a seminar in Seattle with many other Matrix Energeticists we were asked to use Radionics as part of our practice.

My understanding is that in the usual use of Radionics you are finding one vibrational pattern that is causing problems, and then identifying another pattern (or the same reversed or inverted) to cancel the unwanted one.

Knowing that everything that exists is comprised of such patterns (dances of various complexity) and that the same patterns can be carried by thought, light, and sound, I wondered if a more complex pattern could be generated by sound which would be more precise in canceling out more than just one unwanted pattern.

I am not a musician, but I have seen pianists at work. So I connected to the morphic field of music, and asked if my hands could play an imaginary piano to create the desired vibrational pattern in music, and transmit it by thought (or light) to the healee.

I found that I was playing an organ - and the person on whom I was working said afterwards that she felt as if she was in a cathedral! I later asked who had helped, and I was told that it was the organist who worked with Vivaldi when he composed music for the organs of cathedrals.

I now use this instead of finding the correct numbers on dials - and have found it to be faster and more effective.

I suggest that you do this by linking to the morphic fields of organists, of Radionics, and of healing and work with your Heart (linked to the Heart of the healee) so that your hands are used to create the needed vibrational pattern to help the healee with whom you are working.

Experiences

Radionics are a focusing portal that has a morphic field, just as the 2-Pointing, time travel, parallel dimensions/worlds, archetypes, frequencies, clipboard, and all the level four ideas, are focusing portals one has available to allow one's imagination to play and have fun getting the conscious mind occupied so the other than conscious mind (or grace if you prefer) can do all the real work.

Radionics, as far as I understand, is a specific way to use frequencies. The theory is that everything wanted and unwanted are made up of specific energy frequencies.

Using an imaginary Radionics machine is like a 2-Point between what is wanted and what is unwanted; it is like dis-creating what is unwanted by inverting or reversing the direction of the wave frequency back on itself - to cancel itself out.

A lot of energy processes work from this principle such as most of the Spiritual Technology process and other polarity modalities.

Most technology that gets results, as far as I can tell has this principle involved even if the practitioner or even the teacher is not aware of it.

How to use a virtual Radionics machine

Think of a particular issue/problem/challenge as a radio station sending out a signal (light and information) and what you are going to do is put a small sample of the issue/problem/challenge on your virtual Radionics machine. Then you are going to turn the dial until it feels right; when it feels right you have found the frequency, and broadcast it back to the issue/problem/challenge to dis-create it.

Now that can show up in a lot of different ways when you get your imagination really going. A focusing portal is a great way of putting it.

The boxes I use have a portal within them where I place things that I am playing with - they do not have to be things per se. They can be an emotion or resistance to something, for instance.

If they show up as objects or symbols then I put the objects into the Radionics machines for the angels to dial in.

My machines look like huge old-time computers with lots of dials and meters on them, and have boxes recessed within them where I place whatever I am working on.

I have gone nuts with Radionics.

I have been putting everything and everyone in Radionics boxes.

One day, an Angel showed up and offered her services to dial in the frequencies on the Radionics box; I have been working so ever since.

Sometimes, more than one Angel shows up to help depending on the size of the job.

Using a Radionics box, thinking I am a bored certified psychic surgeon, I operate on people giving them new organs, new backs, new brains. Why bother washing them - most prefer new rather than refurbished !

I time travel forward to get new exciting 'Matrix Farmasuiticals', and time travel back to when my client was happy and had happy neck, shoulder, etc.

Using Radionics you can assign the radiation a token number that would stand for it's unique vibrational pattern, such as 4, rather than having to find actual numbers. Then test for the same quality as a 4, in the things you are researching. As far as quantity, give yourself a number scale for that, such as 1-100.

If you would like to test your skill or ability for detecting radiation in a real world way just find a cancer chat and volunteers to get your feedback.

That level of radiation is easy to detect and kick start your confidence for other quests. Use a human outline silhouette, general timeline and the screen name you should have no problem. If you can visualize try that route.

It's the body you want to check not the aura. I have done this many times - it works for me, no matter if the subject is inanimate or animate. Perhaps this is like Dowsing for minerals!

Use Organic Radionics - with the Heavenly Organist

Chapter 11

Having a Real Bad Day?
Tap Meridians - Bad gone Away

Tapping Troubles Away

Understanding 'The Matrix'

In 1944, Max Planck, the father of quantum theory, shocked the world by saying that this 'matrix' is where the birth of stars, the DNA of life, and everything between originates - a place where all things begin, the place of pure energy that simply 'is'. In this quantum incubator for reality, everything is possible.

The MATRIX provides:
- The container for the universe
- The bridge between your imagination and your reality
- The mirror in our world for what you create in your beliefs

This link in our understanding is missing in many people.

To tap the force of this matrix, we must understand how it works and speak the language that it recognizes - the secret of the Divine Matrix, as found in the coded language of our cherished traditions and verified in today's science

The Matrix connects us as ONE. When we have a thought, it goes out to the Matrix, and then returns as our life experience.

We can change our lives by changing the thoughts or pictures in the Matrix.

This field or matrix is all around us, and connects us to our past. We hold our traumas and stressful life experiences in the matrix, where they can influence our every thought pattern, behaviour and action. These are held not just as memories but as specific energy bodies, which have been named 'Energy Consciousness Holograms' - the ECHOs in Karl Dawson's 'Matrix Re-imprinting' work.

Sometimes we carry around pictures in our minds from the past, for years. At the time the event occurred, part of the self splits off and goes into the Matrix. It is a dissociated part, a fragment, that becomes an 'Energy Consciousness Hologram', or ECHO.

Our energy field is still vibrating in alignment with the negative picture or event, so we are 'stuck' in the old, painful memories and pictures that are in the Matrix. We also continue to attract more and more negative experiences, because experience follows energy vibration.

Emotional Freedom Techniques (EFT)

Gary Craig developed a magnificent system of tapping on meridian points whilst talking about existing problems and then being free of them.

This is not the place to go through EFT in detail - an excellent synopsis is available on the Holistic Intuition Society's website; go to   www.in2it.ca   and click on 'Tap Troubles Away' to download the free .pdf file on using EFT.

You can also find many videos on EFT using UTube.

Karl Dawson has developed a wonderful system to change old, painful memories and pictures into becoming happy and beneficial - this aspect seems to be ignored by most systems that work with timelines.

Karl's system is an advance on the basic EFT methods, but is still very easy to follow.

Karl has written a book 'Matrix Reappointing using EFT' ISBN 9781848502499 published by Hay House and available on Amazon.

In his DVD series Karl tells how such a change has an effect not just on the person directly affected, but also on the others involved. This can be expected to be of great help to those now dis-incarnated who were associated with the events. I consider that these DVDs to be far superior to the book, and highly recommend them.

One of my friends watched Karl's DVDs, stopping the play every few moments so that she could do the work as shown; the report was that beneficial changes occurred immediately.

In one episode Karl taps on a single meridian point for a few minutes - this brought past life problems to the surface, so that they could be healed and not cause problems in the present (or any future) life.

Again the key was to see, hear, or feel the cause of the major past life trauma involved (usually at death) and to change the record in the matrix / Akashic records to be happy and beneficial. Such a change has an healing effect on not just the person, but also all others involved in that episode.

Another use of such tapping is to tap directly onto a pain - and then set your awareness on to it, so that you can see, hear, or even feel the pain more intensely - for a short time only! Then you can communicate with the pain for healing.

Communicating with Pains

It is most important to treat the pain (and its causes) with kindness, compassion, and love; this may seem a difficult task, but to do the needed healing you must be a friend - not an enemy or victim.

The pain may be associated with a trauma in the present or past life, be due to an emotion such as fear, anger, hate, or jealousy, or be caused by a possessing entity or fragment - in which case exorcism may be needed, as described in my book 'Holistic Exorcism'. It may even be coming to you for healing because you are a healer.

Following are a few suggestions for use in communication - you may have better ones to use, as guided by your Intuition, according to the type of cause, such as entity, fragment, ECHO, or even inter-dimensional beings.

It is also possible that devices have been installed by dark forces or extraterrestrials.

Send True Holy Love, Namaste to the pain and ask :
- Do you have a name ? (may not if not born, etc.)
- Are you related in this present life ? In a past life ?
- Does you have a shape, if so what shape ? Ditto colour, smell.
- What is your intent ?
- What are you trying to do ?
- Were you given a job ? If so, was this job given by those that are 'In the Light' ?
- What do you want for yourself ?
- Would you like to be free of all hurts, pains, and suffering ?
- Would you like to be happy and joyful all the time ?
- Were you 'In the Light' at any time before ?
- So go back in time to when 'In the Light', when first formed ?
- How does this feel ?
- Do you want to keep feeling good, to be in the Light in all eternities ?
- Would you like this to happen now ?
- Do you want to be with your family, friends, in Heaven ?
- Look upwards - can you see Light ? Even a tiny spot ?
- Can you see Angelic Beings or friends or relations nearby ?
- Go now and join with them, in the Light.

Working with Fragments / ECHOs

These may have been afraid to return due to a trauma, a dark entity, or a soul attachment that caused them to leave - these should have been healed already - perhaps by exorcism; if any are still there then heal as outlined below. Each fragment has a cord that still connects to their being.

Fragments of others that have attached are to be returned to their own being; those of the person are to rejoin in the present now.

Send True Holy Love, Namaste to the fragment, and ask:
- Do you have a name ? (may not if not born, etc.)
- Who did you fragment from ?
- When did you join or attach to this person ?
- What is your intent ? What are you trying to do ?
- What do you want for yourself ?
- Do you want to be free of all hurts, pains, and suffering ?
- Do you want to be happy and joyful all the time ?
- If from another person: (dead or alive) (may be a thought form)
- Go now and rejoin that person with True Holy Love, Namaste.
- If problem, do healing on that person, or send directly into the Light.
- Do you now know that your person has been healed and is free of the old problems ?
- Can you now trust the person (as a grown-up) ?
- Now rejoin your person in True Holy Love, Namaste.

It is important to record any changed circumstances in the Matrix/Akashic Record.

Baby Souls

When a baby is conceived but not born (or dies young) its Spirit Consciousness often fragments due to the trauma of death and attaches to the mother; if another baby is conceived it may then 'join' with the new baby soul - this may result in an extra strong male or female personality (if the souls are of the same sex) or to a lesbian/gay adult should the baby souls have different sexual orientations.

If the baby soul remains attached to the mother then the mother can expect problems in later life - and without any realization that a baby soul is involved. For more information read 'A Cry from the Womb' by Gwendolyn Awen Jones (ISBN9780974073019) outlined in my book 'Holistic Exorcism'.

Typical Symptoms of Possession

Include a lack of energy, weakness in the body, severe depression, disturbed thoughts, and/or irrational thinking. In general a person who is possessed can be identified as being extremely negative and severely depressed - especially if anti-social behaviour is exhibited.

Indications of possession include:

Strong negativity
Deep depression
Rapid mood changes
Uncontrolled temper
Self inflicted harm

Even one or two of these indicators may be a signal of possession.

Types of Possession

In using the term 'Possession' we include also the negative influences originating from those who are still alive in the physical plane of existence - their hateful thoughts, curses, and hexes.

Most common are the attachments of Souls (or their fragments) from deceased relatives - including the Souls of children who were not born or died young, and the earthbound parts of family members (and close friends) who have not ascended in the correct manner and seek to continue their earthly existence by invading relatives still alive, especially young children.

Such fragments will often hide in the muscles of the victim; the more developed will also move around within the muscle system - usually the medical professions find that their medicines are not effective in healing the pains. They say "it is all your imagination!"

Worse possession, however, comes from the invasion of deceased addicts when protection is low from drugs or alcohol; and by earthbound Souls (or those who have lost their way) when the subject is unconscious - due to an accident, or especially when under anaesthetics in a hospital.

Even the best of intent from a deceased family member (such as a parent meaning to help a child) can have most unfortunate side effects. Very often the subject then suffers from illnesses brought in to their own body by the deceased relative - sometimes immediately, or perhaps at the age when the 'donor' died!

It is a common occurrence to take on the illness of a possessing spirit entity - hence the usual poor health of a person who is possessed; even a child will reflect poor health when a spirit entity becomes attached.

A person whose physical illness has been medically diagnosed as imaginary may well be the victim of possession! To further complicate the case a person may have several possessing spirit entities 'on board', each having different illnesses and symptoms.

As a result, the victim goes from doctor to doctor, usually getting diagnoses that conflict.

Earthbound spirits (usually the surviving consciousness of deceased humans) are the most prevalent possessing, obsessing or attaching entities to be found.

The disembodied consciousness seems to attach itself and merge fully or partially with the mind of a living person, exerting some degree of influence on thought processes, emotions, behavior and the physical body.

The entity becomes a parasite in the mind of the host. A victim of this condition can be totally amnesic about episodes of complete takeover.

Most people are vulnerable to spirit attachment on many occasions in the normal course of life. Some investigators in this field estimate that between 70% and 100% of the population are affected or influenced by one or more discarnate spirit entities at some time in their life (Berg, 1984, p. 50; Fiore, 1987b).

Any mental or physical symptom or condition, strong emotion, repressed negative feeling, conscious or unconscious need can act like a magnet to attract a discarnate entity with the same or similar emotion, condition, need or feeling. Anger and rage, fear and terror, sadness and grief, guilt, remorse or feelings of the need for punishment can invite entities with similar feelings.

Severe stress may cause susceptibility to the influence of an intrusive spirit. Altering the consciousness with alcohol or drugs, especially the hallucinogens, loosens one's external ego boundaries and opens the subconscious mind to infestation by discarnate beings. The same holds true for the use of strong analgesics and the anesthetic drugs necessary in surgery.

A living person can have dozens, even hundreds of attached spirits as they occupy no physical space. They can attach to the body or float within the aura. If any part of the body of the host has a physical weakness the earthbound can attach to that area because of a corresponding weakness or injury to the physical body of the spirit prior to death. A spirit can lodge in any of the chakras of the host, drawn by the particular energy of the chakra or by the physical structures of that level of the body.

A living human can be affected by an attached spirit in many different ways. The discarnate entity retains the psychic energy pattern of its own ailments following death and can produce in the host any mental aberration or emotional disturbance and any symptom of physical illness.

In most cases, a person can only experience and acknowledge the reality of the condition after an attached entity has been released. The realization may come some months after a releasement session as the person suddenly notices the absence of a familiar attitude, desire, addiction or behavior.

Read my book 'Holistic Exorcism' for more details

Chapter 12 *We are Energy Beings, and if we Ask We can make Copies to do a Task*

Clones

In tales of Tibetan Buddhism there are reports of people making clones of themselves called 'tulpas' - and that after a few months of existence they can be seen by other people as if real. When they get to such an advanced stage of development it seems most difficult to end them.

It seems that making a clone of oneself involves making a portion of one's Spirit consciousness as a separate consciousness, perhaps in the mental or higher planes, to do a particular job.

I personally ask my Heart to make clones of itself that I send to watch over persons who need exorcism - to watch whatever happens, see whatever is causing problems, and to call in higher levels of energy beings such as Angels to do the required work in healing.

If a person fragments his consciousness in this way, there may be a problem in ensuring that his consciousness is complete and free of fragmentation when death occurs.

I believe that all clones that are made have the knowledge, skills, and abilities of their maker, and are able to obtain more from the Matrix and the Angelic Beings as needed - they should be given specific tasks to complete with the intent that they return when their job is done.

I get my Heart clones to report back every day (and more often if requested) to give situation reports so that my Heart is always aware of the causes and actions taken to ensure that healing is given to the extent needed.

Clones can be considered as intelligent thought forms, capable of having their own thoughts - and using these to influence others.

An example of this would be sending one (or more) clones to attend a meeting with the intent to get a certain point of view accepted and the needed action taken.

How does this work? The higher realms are domains of thought, and when thoughts are sent to someone they tend to act on them - although this may not be true if the thoughts conflict with deeply embedded beliefs such as those concerning morals.

This is actually similar to the action of possessing Spirits - including their fragments. Thus it is most important to never misuse a clone - to always assign them tasks which are beneficial to all concerned, never using them just for one's own personal gain such as sexual involvement, greed, jealousy, or any similar outcome.

Remember that what you send out always comes back to you, usually in a more powerful way; it is accepted by many that what you attract to you is the result of your thoughts - 'like attracts like'. So if you would not like something happening to you, do not try to inflict it on others.

Making a Clone

The simplest way is by thought. But you can define a routine such as clapping hands in a certain way, or doing a special dance.

When you use energy to make a clone, that energy can be used by the clone to give it more power to do the given task.

Experiences: The rest of this chapter comprises conversations between some friends - in this typeface, another in this one, *and others in these fonts using italic.*

I think we each develop our little processes. Mine is just a personalized variant on what I was shown/taught in some prior seminar. So this is just my little version of the basic clone creation idea. From the heartspace (absolute key), I simply do a little dance stepping forward on one foot then rocking back on the other, doing this 3 times.

The fourth time, I do the same - depositing my clone with the forward step (but without actually physically taking the steps). I basically watch myself deposit the clone on the fourth rocking step.

Depending upon how many clones I am making, I do this with different feet and in different directions - for example forward left, forward right, backward left, backward right, etc. Doing this from the heart space is absolutely essential for me.

I may have assigned tools/areas for each clone to cover or have them simply work on what shows up for them. My own rule is that they know exactly what to do when I seem stumped.

One possible idea as it shows up for me is to ask for 'useful' vision. You could make a couple of clones and have each 'work in shifts'. Then notice anything different the next 24-48 hours even if it seems completely unrelated to vision.

Acknowledge each difference that you notice and watch for more differences to show up. This could involve anything, from differences in your dreams (number, type complexity) to the taste of your breakfast, to the number of stoplights that are red on the way to work, to a bird call you happen to notice today that you did not hear yesterday. Any difference you might notice !

We tend to want to see changes linearly. But at least for me, they almost never happen that way. The newly noticed bird call might be the route that connects to useful shifts involving vision. In my opinion, to insist on having brain-directed linear relationships show up is unbelievably restrictive and pretty much shuts down the realm of possibilities.

Sometimes I have specific tasks show up for my clones, such as one to ask about parallel universes, another about time travel, another about archetypes. Other times I give no directions to a clone. Instead I simply allow them to each ask among various tools that show up in their awareness.

You might keep in mind that 'restore your vision' is actually rather restrictive. What if your vision shifted more usefully by 1% each day for the next 100 days?

That is actually a different path than 'restore your vision'. It might well be one where you body is more in harmony as well. So my advice might be to just to allow for what is more useful that includes shifts in your vision and allow that to show up however it might.

Keep in mind that the most profound shift you experience could well be when a new Matrix Energeticist practices on you for his/her first time.

The more you play with it and get used to things just showing up, the more they do. My wife and I pretty much expect 'the unexpected' to happen about once a week. It is our own little 'reality' show.

In fact, another possible suggestion for you just showed up as I was typing this - watch for some anomaly. Something that just makes no sense.

Then you will know you are in an altered reality/parallel universe and can start to ask what else is altered there. It is a cool way to see lots of shifts!

For example, a dear experienced Matrix Energeticist guru friend of ours was in a local restaurant-pub and looked outside a window to see an anomaly - a tall man dressed as a cowboy accompanying a well-appointed dwarf woman walking down a sidewalk in the rain - but not getting wet!

The woman paused and looked inside the window straight at our friend as if to say "Are you paying attention?" Our friend immediately knew ... "I'm in a parallel universe, I wonder what else is different and useful here".

A week later a similar anomaly happened to me during an out of town trip.

So do watch for evidence that you have stepped into a place where stuff is different and there might be something useful for you there.

"It appears your clones display 'your innate' intelligence." That is a really interesting and useful observation. They are all me. But perhaps clones can be a 'me' who is paying attention where I am not, or who is unburdened by present worries or attachments.

Of course in contrast, we can also create a clone to do the 'worrying' for us.

We can also have trail-blazing clones to clear a path for us before we visit a store, go to work, attend a meeting, or travel on a trip.

The possibilities for use of clones are basically endless. Here are some examples:

- They can clear your route to work - encounter traffic hazards such as deer before you do in your car.
- A clone can be a scout when you physically cannot go to certain location.
- If you have a lecture, send a clone ahead to condition and hold space in the auditorium preceding the lecture.

Essentially, my presence is there getting things ready for a useful lecture while I am still showering and enjoying eating breakfast.

With the travel we do, when we are separated my wife and I can actually sense each others' clone in the room and in bed with us.

In fact more than once, I forgot to tell my wife I was sending a clone; the next morning she would telephone to say "you sent a clone last night and he was right there with me, how nice!" We both sleep better, its comforting, and our stress levels are lower.

If I do not sleep well one night, I can leave a clone in bed to refresh while I go to work. In potentially contentious meetings, I will often place clones at the corners of the room or behind each participant to hold space.

It is only to facilitate a useful outcome, not to heavy-hand any particular agenda. But it has resulted in people who have previously taken stands 180 degrees opposite to mine inexplicably changing their position in the meeting and even adopting words/phrases that I have previously used.

I returned from one such out-of town meeting and told my wife that I did not even need to be there. They had stated my views much more articulately than I ever could.

Meetings where I use clones usually take far less time than allocated. In fact academicians love to talk and are often surprised/stunned when such meetings end in half the time they would normally take.

I think that use of the term 'clones' is pretty straightforward. But I suspect people may have used the terms 'Multiple selves' or 'Other selves' to mean at least two different things:

- clones in this parallel - the same as the term 'clones' in ME.
- variants of ourselves that exist in different parallel universes.

For the latter use of other selves, I could have a longer nose in parallel #2, be bald in parallel #3, be more youthful in parallel #4, be dead in parallel #5 (we will skip over that one), or be the same minus some physical complaint in parallel #6, etc.

Okay, I believe I've just stepped into the Twilight Zone. I've been using your suggestions. Last night I had even stranger dreams than I normally do.

One was about Waltzing Matilda; that dream and another one were actually dreams within dreams.

More things disappearing. Tonight since I've been home from work, I've found huge red 'something' covering my hands (it wasn't blood) - and on a paper towel that was totally clean two minutes earlier.

Two huge blobs of this red 'stuff' soaked into the paper towel (about 2" x 2"). There is no 'physical source' for where it came from either time - it just appeared.

My hands still have a little on them even after washing several times. So I asked what else is different.

That's awesome ! Great idea to take a photo so your left brain cannot logic that away and it just gives up.

The dream within a dream sounds rather like the 'Inception' movie - which, by the way, is the music we often use before we do a matrix session with clients. I wonder if you are drilling down in yourself to find and unravel some not-so-useful pattern.

The 'clone in the bed' is probably not my most successful use of clones, to date. But I put it out there because it is likely to work well for others.

I strongly urge developing your own personalized tweaks/ protocols on this as they show up for you in the heart space.

When I am at home and have a bad night with very little sleep, I often forget to use a clone. After dragging a couple of hours at work I will often install a module to address that.

When I do remember to use the 'clone in bed' tool, it does work. But, for me, it works best only after my clone has actually spent some time sleeping during the day.

So the biggest difference I notice is that towards the end of the work day and as I get back home, I am relatively refreshed and in much better shape than when I left for work absolutely dragging.

I probably need to back date the time my clone started sleeping for an earlier-in-the-day effect. I also use 'clone in the bed' for minimizing time involved with jet lag, although even there I tend to remember to use it on the 'away from home' travel leg more than when I am arriving back home.

When you arrive in a great place and do not want to sleep for two days with jet lag when you could be out doing things, put a clone in bed and go out to start your sightseeing or work.

I do not know if anyone except my wife has ever visually seen my clone. My going invisible is what others have definitely observed - including once at a seminar in Seattle. But what I do notice is that the 'effects' of having clones present in a forum are commented on by others.

For example, last spring I sent clones into meeting in DC where I was concerned about the agenda - it seemed like the participant list was designed for an specific outcome, to stonewall change, and not one I might view as useful.

I sent in clones with no agenda beyond whatever would be useful, and then had participants comment to me afterward. As reflected in the minutes, the issues I would have raised had I been physically present at that forum were predominant in the deliberations. So the effect was that I was there.

I did describe exactly how I make mine using a little dance. I think I modified it from a bunny hop that someone in the seminar taught me - its a little less obvious when I do my dance in public!

I think the main keys are to be in the heart space and use whatever little technique shows up for you as a method. For example, in the spirit of a Whizzard class, I imagine someone could simply rotate their forearm from palm down to up and say 'Voila' to create a clone as well.

More about the mysterious red substance that appeared yesterday. I still have remnants on my hands - very light, but enough to remind me it was real. Plus I have the photo of the paper towel. And I didn't tell you about the smell of the paper towel.

I had been using the paper towel as a napkin. That's how I know the huge red spots had not been there two minutes earlier. When I noticed it and saw there was no place that the substance could have come from either time, I sniffed the paper towel. It smelled a little like ink, but not really. It seemed like a familiar scent though.

Today I am wondering if that substance is something that my body is releasing in order to create change with my glaucoma and vision difficulties.

I really physically do the dance and that is very important for me. My own dance is probably not quite as silly looking as if I did the prototype bunny hop but it is silly enough to be perfect as one of my ME tools.

It is like a variant on swing dance steps. and on what would be the fourth rocking forward step - when I do not physically step forward - I see my clone step out of me. My left brain has no excuse but to accept it because it is a silly (but very high) ritual.

More on clones. I had a meeting at work this morning where I take notes. This particular group tends to just 'blah-blah-blah' for most of the meeting, with no real issues mentioned.

So before the meeting I placed four clones in the corners of the room to speed things up. It went well for a while and the meeting was just about over, when the Human Resources person started up - he really loves to hear his own voice. So I placed more clones around the room.

I placed one behind each person at the table. It did speed people up to finish sooner. A lot of topics were covered and we finished in 34 minutes, which is almost a record.

How wonderful. I find that despite the meetings actually ending sooner, everyone seems to feel like they had input and that is was a better than normal use of their time.

I had a similar example of that last week where a two hour scheduled meeting took 55 minutes. The participants literally did not know how that happened - or what they would do, as they departed the meeting, with the hour-plus unallocated time they now had.

I have spent multiple sessions hanging out with other versions of myself. Just last night I flew with a far alternate version who had wings. Perhaps this is where I get dreams of flying. My clone's reply was that now he knew where he got dreams of walking !

Way too much fun !

The further off the current probability stream you go, the wilder the differences. Some streams must have diverged millennia ago.

I did a little dance similar to the way that you describe to make a clone and sent it ahead in the restaurant where I go to scope out where I should best sit, since where I was sitting the day before ended up making me upset - due to the people around me.

I started to walk to the restaurant and before I got there though the clone has chosen a different spot.

I got to the restaurant and it was quiet where my clone had chosen.

I sat there and ordered something totally different for breakfast than my normal.

In the afternoon my clone had chosen another different spot - the same crowd was in, and in same sort of mood as yesterday, but I was not sitting near them this time since my clone did its job.

While I was at work I was trying to decide if my version of the little dance would work, when a different method showed up.

You spoke of it being just silly enough to bypass your left brain. I work with children and am known a lot as the 'silly teacher'. What showed up is flicking my wrist 3 times while my hand turns from down to up, like you do while your doing the hokey pokey.

On the third flick up and picturing the fourth time while saying "Ta Da" there was the clone. I was practicing that in the class subtlety today, and made a whole line of clones.

I do this with the fun and innocence of a child; when we are doing the hokey pokey together, singing and being silly I was unsure which method I should use.

I suspect though that this will not be the end of ideas on how to make clones!

The clones are yours and it is your 'rules' for both their creation and their use - as with any Matrix Energeticist technique.

Remember I said that one of my rules is that when I am stumped, my clones know exactly what to do. So your clones do not have to be unduly burdened by holding and working with any particular pattern unless that is part of your rule set.

You have to be congruent with using clones in this way - and the possibility they can hold or handle what you may have struggled to overcome - or at least they can work with this pattern and give you an opportunity to see what shows up when you are free of holding it.

It could be just having a clone hold the pattern for a while that allows you to walk around it and get a new perspective on working with or shifting the pattern.

It is best to use this clone tool only if you are congruent with its use; but you also have aids like Frequency 3 that can help to harmonize you to any tool.

Perhaps there are aspects of a pattern that at least one part of you does not want to relinquish - even to a clone. You might ask about that from the heart space, and/or separate those parts out so you only assign a clone to hold and work through one part of the larger pattern.

I had another experience with clones. I decided before entering my class room to make a clone to stand or sit by each of my 9 toddlers in my class. The purpose was to make the class room calmer and quieter, and to get the children to fall asleep quicker.

So on my I did my version of the little dance down the nine stairs to my classroom, each clone entering the class and then went to each child.

By the time I made it to the bottom of the stairs the classroom was quieter then usual, and the children then went to their beds. It took less time for the children to fall asleep.

I was thinking that if one is vulnerable and raw working with intense grief, perhaps clones could be friends that help to carry the burden of something by listening and being there for us.

This got me thinking. If clones are us as we are in this reality, don't they also have our limitations?

Would it be better to ask an alternate self to deal with stuff we feel we cannot handle than to ask a clone, which could also feel that it cannot?

From what I have understood, that doesn't seem to be the case. So I'm wondering perhaps clones and alternative selves are illusions - why not, if everything else is!

Can we achieve these things without either? In other words, perhaps using them gets our left brain out of the way just as other things we do when working with the Matrix, but ultimately they have nothing to do with the results.

In no way do clones have to have our limitations unless that is part of one's personal rule set. We each create our own clones and we each make the rules under which they operate. If one chooses to address limitations one could work it either way.

Either the clone can go where we might be limited (i.e. our clones know what to do, even when we do not) or I could ask a clone to hold on to my limitations while I am free of them for a period.

Same potential of enlarged possibilities.

Regardless of how they start, the minute they are doing something I am not doing, they are no longer exactly like me. They are then a different aspect.

I like to think of them as clones because in the split second they come out, they are identical - but not the next split second.

In one interesting occasion I was in a pretty heightened Heart Space state and thought I would go into the first (nearest) men's room - until I altered my steps at the last second when I saw the lineup protruding out of the door.

So I was in the Heart Space, directed my motion toward the door and essentially dance stepped away.

My wife saw the motion and 'me' continue on into the first men's room. The conditions were pretty similar to how I make my clones. I was just surprised I was not focused on doing that - but I was not at all surprised it had happened.

They are also in this universe, whereas, my 'other selves' are in parallel universes (e.g. the one whose is bald or the one who has a longer nose) and are not identical.

I should add that regardless of what they are called, the important thing is that they are aspects of you in this universe that you create to aid you - and you set their rules of operation.

On the grief aspect, I want to elaborate a bit more on some possible ideas that have helped me personally.

You may find that it is only a part of what can be a large grief pattern that you want to sublet to a clone. For example you could have the recent personal pattern intertwining with huge ancestral patterns - just using that as an example.

So if this shows up for you, don't hesitate to break out a part of the grief pattern you are presently holding and let the clone help with that.

Some huge intense patterns are easy to tackle and shift in pieces (plus your left brain understands that approach) or maybe 20% of the grief pattern is not ready to shift. So you can always ask about what part of it could be assigned to a clone for it to hold and work on.

The clones are yours and it is your 'rules' for both their creation and their use - as with any technique.

Remember I said that one of my rules is that when I am stumped, my clones know exactly what to do. So your clones do not have to be unduly burdened by holding and working with a grief pattern unless that is part of your rule set.

My clones are whole body replicas. Not just a part. Making the clone is a personalized and individual thing. Probably the only thing in common is that it is done from the heart space. The way I do it is not the way my wife does it - or possibly anyone else. There is nothing inherently magical about my dance other than it works well for me. We each find a way that makes sense to us.

To me, I do the three little rocking steps (like part of a dance), and on the fourth, my clone takes the step but I stand still and only watch. The clone essentially steps out of me - and I observe and acknowledge it.

Are clones doppelgangers?

That may well depend upon the frame of reference or point of view. I think they are what we make them.

Usually my clones are not actually seen and are only 'detectable' by others via the work they do. So a client will comment on what they felt, noticed, or perceived as a clone 'worked' on them.

While you certainly could be specific (at least what you expect the clones to do), I tend to leave it as wide open as possible since many useful outcomes were never what I had envisioned beforehand. Perhaps your meeting did not need much tweaking? Did it go OK in the end?

Has any meeting aftermath been something you might notice as different? One of our friends has noticed that a meeting did not seem to change, but the people in it started acting differently toward her, such as voluntarily helping her more after the clone-tweaked meeting.

I found it interesting that our friend adjusted his clones during the class and after that he really started noticing stuff. You might try experimenting with using your clone in meetings and see what gives you easily noticeable effects. See if shuffling them around mid meeting does anything? I think we each develop our own little protocols.

I would encourage you to try not being too specific on outcomes or even detailed processes. If you go for 'what is useful' and leave it wide open you may get results that are wonderful - but that you had never envisioned.

Watch for different things showing up during the 48 hours after clone-influenced meetings. That is what one of our friends notices more often than shifts in meeting behavior.

I just gave the pattern to the clone with 'I don't know how to work with this to transmute it to be different but trusting you do' and then trusted that the clone knew what to do - and how to do it.

I absolutely love that approach. I do the same thing with my clones when I am unsure what to do. My own little rule is that they do know when I do not. 'No muss, no fuss' as my mother used to say.

I like the understanding that "you do not have to create the reality you desire, because it already exists". I am coherent with this statement, and I just have to become a vibratory match to it - and then step into it.

Whether you call something a clone who happens to differ from you in a moment because it is assigned to hold something you released, or is doing something, or is in 'a different parallel you' is strictly related to what process you are using - as it showed up for you.

There is no right way or wrong way if it shows up for you in the heart space.

I have a personal example from yesterday of an event or process being open to multiple possible explanations or interpretations.

I ran an errand to a hardware store chain and arrived back home while my wife was in the back yard with our dog. The dog always barks when she hears somebody on another part of the property. I shut the car door and checked the front door - and found that I could not enter since the screen door was locked from the inside.

After calling for my wife unsuccessfully, I walked through a 5-6 ft wide breezeway and entered via the backdoor.

During this time, my wife heard a car door slammed, then she heard a car drive up in the driveway - a reversed process from what was normal/expected.

That should have been a clue this was going to get interesting! Always watching the breezeway (near the back door) my wife walked through the breezeway to the end and she saw the car - but not me! Then she reversed and went back to the backyard though the breezeway still watching the backdoor and breezeway.

The next thing she knew I was calling to her from upstairs inside the house. It was seemingly impossible for us to have not encountered each other - if not actually to run into each other. We had to have passed by each other in the 5-6 ft wide breezeway or crossed visual paths just a few feet away.

Was it invisibility, or were we in different parallel universes? We have discussed it several times and simply don't know. It could have been either or something we have not yet considered.

Chapter 13   *Time and Space may be an Illusion*
We can Navigate to stop Confusion

Lords of Time and Space

We all have the ability to be Lords of Time and Space - well, most of us do. There is one part of us that always works in the 'NOW' - our sub-conscious mind.

This has some great advantages - and some serious drawbacks.

As we repeat an action (or emotion) it is stored in our sub-conscious memory for future reference, and the more that an action is repeated the stronger it is reinforced in our memory banks.

When a situation arises, our sub-conscious searches our memory for a similar situation that is stored, and if found it automatically repeats the action taken before. An example is learning to ride a bicycle.

This is of great help in handling an emergency situation, because the action is taken immediately; it is done without reference to our logical mind-brain.

This often causes a serious problem - we react without thought, even though the reaction is not what we would take if the situation was properly considered.

Our sub-conscious memory banks started in the womb, when we relied on the thoughts of our mother - and also picked up thoughts from others who were in contact with our mother. This continued as an infant and as a child, extended to those who were in contact with us directly.

So our sub-conscious became accustomed to taking all that was said by others as being 'The Truth'. What we personally thought was of lesser value, and often ignored - hence we usually have little ability to change what is in our sub-conscious memory banks.

Hypnotism often works because we are guided to understand that what is told is said by others and is therefore true.

Self hypnotism can also help in correcting mis-conceptions in our sub-conscious, and NLP (Neuro Linguistic Programming) with 'Trigger Points' is also effective in many cases.

The most effective methods are those outlined by Gary Craig's EFT (Emotional Freedom Technique) where the time of the 'First Cause' is found and then 'tapped away'; by 'Quantum Jumping' (developed by 'The American Monk', Burt Goldman); and in ME where travel is made to different times and/or universes.

Such travel involves finding when and where the cause did not happen, installing this memory in the sub-conscious memory banks to over-ride the unwanted ones that contained the cause, and returning to the present - usually taking a different path to avoid any re-installation of the unwanted cause.

Our sub-conscious has a very important job - to protect us. If something 'not good' happened, the circumstances involved are stored with PRIORITY.

This is the major source of allergies - often the true cause of a problem is not recognized, but the substance associated with the happening is taken as being the cause.

If you took an action that caused harm to your self (or others) then your sub-conscious may send you hurts and pains to teach you a lesson - and in almost all cases you fail to associate 'The Punishment' with 'The Crime'. This is not your fault - the places and types of hurts, pains, and illnesses seem to be chosen in an arbitrary manner that is foreign to our logical mind-brain.

In a similar way a 'hex' or 'curse' set on a person is implemented by the sub-conscious. It is sent by another, so it 'must be true'. It may need the help of a 'different other' to clear it and to heal the damage already caused. Thus in some cases getting help from another Healer is more effective than working on oneself.

As a Lord of Time and Space you find when and where you need to go, take the healee there with you (in your imaginative mind), change the circumstances (perhaps in stages), and then return to the present via a different route, so avoiding incidents that would influence the new paradigm in a negative way.

Time Travel

The basic intent is to determine when the 'First Cause' of a problem occurred, to go to just before that occurrence, overlay the present sub-conscious with the memories before the occurrence, and return with these to the present time.

You may be able to do this by just asking "Please take the person to the time of the 'First Cause' of (the problem)", and check if this is now so; if not, then you have to find that time in another way.

Using mathematical techniques, identify a key point (such as birth) and ask "Did this happen before the birth of this person in this lifetime?".

If YES, then you are dealing with past life stuff, so ask "More than 100 past lives?" etc. until you get NO. For example, if 100 gave a YES and 200 a NO, you know that it was between 100 and 200 - so divide in two, and ask "More than 150?". If YES, the range is between 150 and 200, so ask "More than 175?".

If the first answer was NO, then you are dealing with the current life, so ask "After birth?" - if NO then search in months over the period between conception and birth, such as "After 5 months?"; if YES, then choose an age such as half the present age (66) of the person as your start point (33) and narrow it down in the same way as previously mentioned.

Example: 33+? YES; 45+? NO; 39+? NO; 36+? YES; so it is 37, 38, or 39; 37+? NO; Check: Is it 37? YES.

You can use your Pendulum to get these YES or NO answers - my preferred method is to use my tongue as the indicator, as previously mentioned in the chapter on Kinesiology and Dowsing.

This is the way that I determine the depth of a water vein and the flow of water in the vein when Dowsing for wells.

Another way is to draw a line to scale (or on squared paper) and Dowse with your Pendulum for the age. You can also feel with your finger on the line, or imagine in your mind's eye a dial which is turned to the age.

The examples below will use both archetypes and time travel. Utilizing multiple ME tools simultaneously allows you greater flexibility to achieve the desired result.

Experiences

Without further adieu, here's some stories by Matrix Energeticists to illustrate the different ways to use time travel.

Let your imagination be free! There are no rules!! Play with the freedom of a happy child!!!

When time-traveling, I see both my client and I going back to the day just before whatever has caused some undesirable condition in the present. When we're back in that time, we overwrite the client's present state in the past and return to the present.

Find the Real Cause

A woman came in coughing, sneezing and blowing her nose. On the surface, common cold or some such ailment.

Always focus on the little man behind the curtain and not the great and terrible Oz. In other words, find out what's really going on in stead of taking situations at their face value.

After discussing her week, we discovered that her new supervisor was blaming her for everything that was going wrong. Some things she said her supervisor told her to do and after she did it, she was asked why she did that. Her main lament was, "It was never like this in all the years I've been there."

She has worked in the accounting department of one of the oldest hotels in the area for the last 32 years.

We moved back in time to the day before her first day there. We overwrote her knowledge of how it's always been, with how she felt before she even started there. Once in this new-old state of I don't know what to expect so I'll be ready for anything, we returned to the present.

As a side note, to do this, I usually create a 'PRESENT TIME' button on my control panel. When I'm done in the time period I traveled to, I press it and return to the present.

Anyway, when we returned to the present and she came to, most of her cold symptoms were gone. Moved her to an alternate universe where she has forgiven her supervisor and the rest of the symptoms were gone.

Significant Event Method

I was driving along in my 1994 Mazda Truck when it started making this loud squealing noise. I figured I could make it home, but just in case, I 2-Pointed the truck steering wheel and envisioned my truck safe and sound backed into my drive way.

About 30 seconds later, the engine died and I rolled off to the side of the road and called AAA. About an hour later, there was my truck, just as I had envisioned it, safe and sound backed into my drive way.

I isolated the problem to my air conditioning compressor. It sounded like the bearings were shot. What a perfect opportunity to use time travel! I 2-Pointed the compressor and envisioned a wall clock in my mind's eye. I watched the clock hands go backwards two hours. I started the truck and it began to squeal away. OK, so that didn't work. I began to wonder when were the bearings fine. Then I thought well, in 1994, the bearings should have been fine. But when in 1994? What if this was a 1994 that was built in 1993? So after some deliberation, I decided on the first time the first owner first turned on the air conditioner.

Now I don't know when that event took place, but I do know that whenever that was, the air conditioning system was working fine. I 2-Pointed the compressor again and moved us both back to the exact moment when the first owner turned the air conditioner on. After everything settled (I stopped swaying), I started it up and it worked fine.   Turned the air conditioner on and everything was cool!

Be specific with your intentions: Instead of just envisioning a positive outcome, include how you arrive at the positive outcome. I should have seen myself driving the truck home under its own power and parking it in my drive way.

Use specific events or times as a focal point. By focusing on a specific event, I can place my client in that specific frame. Whatever is happening then is what we have happening now. Even if I have no idea when that event occurred, as long as I know it did happen, I am able to use it.

<u>Calendar Method</u>

A young girl came in on a Thursday, complaining of congested lungs and sinuses and a sore throat. This was especially troubling for her because she was going to be singing a solo in a community musical the following Sunday!

I asked her mother when all the symptoms started and she said it started when she got up on Monday morning. This is the 'Zero Point Reference' that Dr Bartlett discusses in his book.

I established my standard 2-Point and pictured in my mind's eye, a calendar with a red box on Thursday, to represent that day. I moved the red box back day by day to Monday and nothing happened. I moved the red box back to Sunday and the girl started swaying in a circle. While she was swirling, I quietly asked her mother what happened Sunday. She said rehearsal and it didn't go well. I asked why not and she said that her voice cracked during her solo and after that she couldn't really sing that song at all.

I silently asked where in the song her voice cracked and I saw a line with a lump in it near the end. I silently asked if the lump in the line is where her voice cracked, and I heard a reply that said "it's too hard and I can't". I asked the girl to sing the end of the song in her head over and over again until I told her to stop.

Silently again, I asked everything making the lump appear in the line to clear. More swaying. Big circles at first and then smaller and smaller, until she just sat back. Since I couldn't see the lump anymore, I moved the red box forward on the calendar until we were back to the Zero Point (Wednesday). She felt a little dizzy, so I centered, grounded and balanced her. Sinuses, lungs and throat were all clear of all symptoms.

Use familiar tools: Instead of just counting backwards through the days, I used a calendar.

In this case, I only needed to go back three days, but sometimes the cause starts months or years before the manifestation of the symptom. A calendar is helpful for moving through months and even years by simply flipping a page back, like in a cartoon.

<u>Time Machine Method</u>

A man came in at the urging of his wife, daughters and niece. Actually they have been after him to come in for awhile but he was fine, didn't need any help with anything and they didn't know what they were talking about. Three days prior to coming in, he was in a fender bender. Two days prior to coming in, he got in a screaming match with a co-worker. In and of itself, those events themselves weren't very significant. His reactions during the events scared him enough that he figured out he wasn't as fine as he thought. The accident occurred because the vehicle he hit disappeared until it reappeared crunched up in his right front fender. During the shouting match at work he was watching himself yell at his co-worker and wanted to stop but he just couldn't.

Since his family had been after him to come in for awhile, I wanted to know just how old this pattern of behavior actually was.

I established my standard 2-Point and moved us both into a time machine (more like Jules Verne than Doc Brown). I silently asked when was the very first time he felt the way he felt in the last three days. I moved backwards by single years, checking for the answer, until I got to 2000.

Then I started moving backwards by decades, still checking when I stopped. I knew he was in his fifties, so when I got to 1960 and we still hadn't found the first time he felt this way, I continued moving backwards by single years again. I finally got the answer to my question when we hit 1957.

I went back one more year and silently asked if he knew the feeling he was feeling in the past few days and I got NO. I asked him when he was born and he said June 1956. I moved forward in time by months asking when he first felt the feeling and I got March 1957. We backed up to February and jumped out of the time machine. I repeatedly asked him to remember the feelings of this time until he stopped swaying 'round and round'.

Then we jumped back into the time machine and I pressed the Present Time button. This moved us into the exact present time but taking a different path from the one that created the feeling he had been feeling since March 1957.

In other words by creating an alternate reality from the one he grew up in, we avoided the trauma that has literally affected his whole life. After the session, he looked and felt much calmer, but it's what he said later that caught me off-guard. He said that for the first time since he was in his twenties he didn't feel like he needed to get drunk to get to sleep tonight!

Find the root of the current situation: Many problems people have are related and stem from a singular source in the past. By traveling back in time, we can create an alternate reality that stems off of his original reality prior to the trigger event. Avoiding the traumatic trigger event, all of the resulting after effects can also relieved.

Door Method

A woman came in very agitated. Of course, when I asked her how she was feeling and what was going on in her life, she said, "Fine. Nothing." Oookkkaaaaayyyyy. . . After probing a bit we hit on her and her sister planning for their mother's birthday. She was quite angry and expressed that very clearly, once she got started.

For example, she said she had told her sister that she was having invitations printed. Her sister said she could print them if she was given all the information.

Over the next few days, my client proceeded to change everything about how she wanted the invitation, sometimes hourly. Her sister finally told her that she was too busy to print the invitations. My client was very angry, but didn't say anything to her sister. Although she had let that go, she couldn't sleep well every night afterward. She remarked that if she had known she had to do the invitations by herself, then she would have them done by now.

I asked her if she could recall the last time she and her younger sister had a good relationship. She thought for awhile and said they'd never really gotten along since they were children. They are exactly three years apart - born in the same month on the same day. I established my standard 2 point and envisioned a door with the number 30 on it, to represent my client at age 30. I opened the door and asked the 30 year old version of her if she had a good relationship with her sister. She shook her head NO.

I repeated the process at different doors until I arrived at age 4. The little girl nodded yes, indicating she had a good relationship with her sister. This would make her sister 1 year old. In my mind's eye, I entered the 4-year-old room with my client. I asked to have her current relationship with her sister overwritten with a copy of the sister-relationship in the room. She promptly fell to the table and stayed that way for the next 20 minutes. She was still lying on the table and one of her eyes opened. Her gaze was glazed and unfocused.

I 2-Pointed her forehead and said out loud, "You're not done yet."

Her eye closed. 20 minutes later she sat up but was a bit dizzy and felt disoriented. I 2-Pointed her head and her heart and put her in a place where a good relationship with her sister was perfectly normal, comfortable and happy. She swayed a bit and when she opened her eyes, she was focused and clear. She came in the following week and said she had gone home that day and finished the invitations on her own. They came out quite nice, if she did say so herself.

Locate a more positive time: Overwriting a current state with a previous, more positive time allows the client to operate in the present without any emotional baggage from the past.

Walk Through Method

A woman came in very anxious. She was planning to go on a trip with her husband and two children (ages 7 and 5) to Southern California. She was a nervous wreck because she hated riding on planes.

She always got sick and spent most of the flight either knocked out or throwing up or both. She was so riddled with anxiety that she couldn't even go to the website to make her travel arrangements. Every time she even thought about typing in the web address, she got nauseous.

Her good friend is a client of mine and he had been nagging her for the last month to come in. Finally to get him off her back, she agreed to come in but only once. This situation was very complex and she was only coming to see me once. Instead of trying to find a problem point in the past, I decided to do what I call a 'walkthrough'.

In a walkthru you literally walk through every aspect of their trip. Since she hadn't even booked her travel arrangements yet, that was where we were going to start.

I asked her where she kept her computer. She responded that it was in a room that is upstairs and down the hall from her bedroom. I established my standard 2-Point.

Since she described it that way, I asked her to imagine she was at the bottom of the staircase and had her walk up. After two stairs she started swaying ever so slightly and very slowly. By the time we got to the middle of the staircase she was swirling in a large circle. At the top of the stairs, she turned and was now looking straight down the hall and into the computer room. At that point, she fell straight forward almost into her lap.

About ten minutes later she slowly rose back to a seated position and opened her eyes . . . wide! She was a little freaked out but I coaxed her into regaining her composure and we continued on the walkthru. She wobbled and swayed as we continued down the hallway. She started feeling nauseous as we entered the computer room. Once we cleared the nausea away, I had her sit at her desk.

More nausea and some abdominal cramping popped up for clearing. Step-by-step we continued on - turn the computer on, grab the mouse, open your browser, type the web address, search for your travel, car and hotel arrangements, etc. Eventually, we had her sitting with her printed itinerary in her hand and an ear-to-ear smile on her face.

She called two days later and booked several more appointments. She said that she hadn't tried to book her arrangements until today because she couldn't afford to be sick. She finally decided it was now or never and sat down at the computer with no nausea or cramps. She booked her airline, rental car and hotel, got a great discount and still had that nausea-free, cramp-free, ear-to-ear smile.

Rehearse the event and remove all negativity. Clear all of the negativity from an event prior to it happening and create a positive emotional patterning for that future event.

Time travel is a great toy that is easy to use. Don't get too hung up on understanding how it works. Just know it does!

Remember, though, that although ME gives us all of these great toys, your greatest tools are your imagination and the freedom you give yourself - so use it!

Parallel Universes

Parallel universe/dimension, like time travel, is a simple technique but very tricky to wrap you mind around. For simplicity, I'll refer to this toy as parallel universe(s).

Again, like time travel, parallel universes present an opportunity for altering your client's current reality. Instead of finding <u>when</u> things are different, you're finding <u>where</u> things are different.

Now, let's take that one step further. Starting with the moment you are in currently, instead of moving to one and only one next moment in your lifetime or existence, we'll move to one of an infinite number of next moments.

Your choice of action in this current moment, will dictate which of the infinite number of moments or realities you move to next.

So how does this apply for Matrix Energeticists? It allows you to make more positive choices for your client in the current moment. Because of the more positive choice, when you and your client move to the next moment, you are now in a place which is more positive or beneficial for the client. For example, we could go to a moment before the last ball game started, but choose not to play. The next reality or parallel universe you move to, your client never played in the game, and so they never pulled their hamstring.

If we make a different choice in that original decisive moment, then they will move to an alternate reality or parallel universe where the outcome can be different.

Here are some stories to illustrate the different ways I've used time travel and parallel universes.

Experiences of Parallel Universes

Changing the Situation

A woman came in last week. She was cleaning out her storeroom and sprained her thumb. It wasn't swollen anymore, but she couldn't bend it. I established a 2-Point using the base and tip of her thumb.

We first time traveled back to the moment before she started cleaning the storeroom. Next we slid over to a parallel universe where someone else had straightened up and cleaned the storeroom. We brought her forward to the present time in that parallel universe. Her thumb could bend with a little bit of pain, but it could bend.

I found a parallel universe where the storeroom had always been kept immaculate. I reached in a pulled out a copy of her thumb in that parallel universe and replaced her current thumb with the new thumb. She tentatively moved her thumb around but no pain. She bent her thumb to the center of her palm with no pain.

Primary Cause

A woman came in a bit depressed. Since the subject was a bit embarrassing for her, it took awhile for her to explain why she was feeling so down. She was, let's say, less-than-gifted in a womanly way. More directly, an A-cup is a bit loose on her.

I figured it would be easier to boost her self-esteem than change her body shape. After establishing my standard 2-Point, we moved to a parallel universe (or place) where she was comfortable with every aspect of her body.

To move into a new reality, I envision in my mind's eye a glowing circle. I envision it floating over to us and then dropping down on us, starting at our heads and moving down past our feet and in to the floor. Now we are both in the new reality.

Once she was congruent with that new reality, we then moved to a place (parallel universe) where she could see the positive in every aspect of herself. After she settled in, we then moved to a place where she loved every aspect of her body. She left much happier. Since then, she has taken to wearing more age appropriate clothing. She's 27 but her makeup and her dress looked more like that of a 16 year experimenting with drugs and speed metal.

In addition she is smiling a lot more!

Focus on primary causes: Instead of focusing on her breast size, which seemed to be the cause of her depression, we instead focused on her personal perspective. She could see the positive in every aspect of herself, so her physical appearance was no longer an issue.

Common Thread

A boy came in needing help with some of his classes. He was doing poorly, aka getting an "F", in four of his six classes, the worst of which were English and Social Studies.

After talking to him for awhile, we concluded that one of his problems was writing. Basically, he was trying to write in a single draft with no outline, as if he was trying to transcribe the completed product from his head to paper.

Unfortunately, he didn't have the completed paper in his head.

After establishing a basic 2-Point, we moved him to a place where he was very comfortable with all aspects of writing, regardless of the medium (pen & paper, word processor, cell phone, etc.). Once he was in synch with this new reality, we moved, "a little further in and a little deeper down," (I always say this out loud), to a place where he enjoyed expressing his thoughts via the written or typed word.

Once he assimilated this new reality, we moved in to a place where he is a good writer who likes to write. Between each dimensional shift, I would ask him to imagine writing something he had written during the previous weekend. With each move to a new reality, it became easier and easier in his imagination. I suggested re-writing one of the papers that had helped him to earn his current grade and take it to his teacher for evaluation. He smiled and said, "I can do that. I'll do it tonight!"

Discover lowest common denominator: Instead of focusing on the material in each class, we found a common thread that was present in all four classes. By eliminating this thread, we may improve all situations.

Use compound moves: Moving a client to a place where he or she will have to make many complicated emotional shifts might be too difficult for them to handle. Instead, move them through adjoining parallel universes where skill sets or enhancements are slowly added one at a time, which also allows for assimilation in between.

Multiple Layers

A father brought a young boy who came in at his mother's insistence. He's 12 years old and likes eating somewhat like a dog.

He does use utensils, but he liked his plate on the floor and his face about two inches above the plate.

Physically, he sat hunched forward. I could see how eating on the floor might be more comfortable, if one's spine is curved downward.

I asked him why he liked to eat on the floor and he said it was more comfortable. Well, there you go!

After establishing my 2-Point, we moved to a place where it was easier and more comfortable to sit up straight.

Some of the curve released but he was still somewhat slumped over. Still holding the same 2-Point, we time traveled back looking for a time when he naturally sat up straight. Using his body as an indicator, we moved back one year at a time until his body physically shifted. At about 3 years old, he swayed a bit. I then asked everything to do with sitting up straight to overwrite his present settings. After that was complete, we moved back to the present but retaining the new settings.

While integrating all of these changes in to his physical body, he slowly sat up more and more until he was comfortably sitting up straight and tall. He said his head felt "all funny".

I found a parallel universe where he had only always sat up straight. Reached in and grabbed a copy of his head in that parallel universe and plopped it into his head. He felt normal after that.

Multiple causes to a single problem: If something you do only works part-way, don't look at it as a failure. Instead realize that you've assembled part of the puzzle, but there are still a few more pieces to go.

Parallel Universe or Dimension is a great toy that is easy to use. Again, like Time Travel, don't get too hung up on understanding how it works. Just know it does!

Remember, throughout all you do as a Matrix Energeticist, that the limit is always in you. Keep expanding your limits until, for all practical purposes, you have none! In other words be free!

Quantum Jumping

How do you reach the higher mind? How do you become so that you have answers to everything thanks to being able to access everyone's brains, and their knowledge with wisdom?

I'd say the only thing I've seen myself that results in such instantaneous results in IQ and skill gains would be the work introduced by Dr. Vladimir Raikov, demonstrating what he called 'Artificial Reincarnation' through deep hypnosis, where he would tell the person in a very deep trance that he's a genius (like Da Vinci for example) and then asks him to demonstrate that genius skill. He got people to paint like Da Vinci and play violin & piano like masters. After coming off Hypnosis, they'd retain many of the skills they attained.

Burt Goldman does this in his 'Quantum Jumping', where instead of merging with a genius he meets his doppelganger - who is a genius in what he wants to learn and exists in a parallel universe.

Burt learned through it to become a great photographer, started painting incredibly, learned singing, healing, and helped him make his very own lucrative business.

I have been doing a lot of work with Quantum Jumping (QJ) - when you go outside of yourself and visit one of multiples of yourself in another dimension, your 'doppelgangers'.

I am one that does not like rules of any kind so I'm a rule breaker when it comes to this stuff. I had the 3 most explosive energy sessions in my life, the last 2 being that my body vibrated, tingled and pulsed out of my hands and feet for 2 hours and then 3 days afterwards. That was quite a trip!

The 'Exploding Me' exercise: QJ is simple; just sit down and relax yourself by a 10 to 1 count down.

Once in a relaxed state imagine a room with a door; now count down 3 to 0 and place yourself in the room with the door in front of you.

Opening the door would lead you to any 'quantum you' that you are looking for - this is where you place your intention of who you want to see before you open the door and jump.

Now the exploding you part; when you are in the room, place an intention that there is a gap between the door and the reality bubble that exists in front of you.

This is how I see it - the first bubble is the main bubble that holds all of the other 'yous' in your reality, like a balloon with a billion of smaller balloons inside of it.

Your intention is to appear out in space looking at the big bubble, like looking at earth from out in space. Once there call 'Mr Green Fuzzy Photon' for help; at this point allow yourself to break down in to a billion fuzzy green photons; now you can interact with every multiple dimensional of you that exists - all at the same time.

When you are done call yourself back to space and reassemble yourself, then step back through the door, and then count back 0 to 3 to get you back in to your body. You can then take this and make it what ever you want it to be - it is quite brain numbing and intense.

Notes:

Set the Energies to be Free
To Find a Better way to Be
Looking with Good God Grace
In all Time and Space
With True Holy Love, Namaste

Chapter 14

If I want to Help You
This is What I Do

Sending Healing

Modules in years past were information models that were labeled and identified, such as a torsion field module. They were designed for specific purposes - correction, shifting, etc.

Then it was recognized that if we just hold out our hands and request the Matrix to make a module particular for who and what we are playing with, that the Zero Point Field (ZPF) did it to perfection. So we just allow the creation of a module, install, and activate NOW.

Templates are similar, sometimes considered easier to use.

Modules

There is a chapter on modules in Richard Bartlett's book 'The Physics of Miracles'.

A 'module' is a packet of information. It contains everything necessary to address an issue, a disease, a condition, a circumstance, or a situation.

Here's the definition in computer language - "Modular design - the engineering discipline of designing complex devices using separately designed sub-components".

The great thing about modules is that you don't have to design the sub-components - or the module itself. The purpose of modules is to save time and cover all of the bases - without you having to know what's needed.

A basic and powerful method is to:

1. Open in 'True Holy Love' to 'The System' and 'The Matrix' ('The Field').

2. Hold out your hand and ASK for what is needed and beneficial.

3. Let the field CREATE one for you (or whoever is the recipient).

4. INSTALL it wherever it wants to go in or around the body - ask where, or just be guided by your intuition.

5. ACTIVATE it to run whenever it is needed.

When you do this you may feel it in your hand - it fills up, floats down and stops; then install and activate it.

Let the intelligence of the Zero Point Field create the perfect module - and then follow instructions or guidance from your intuition.

Hold out your hand, ask for the perfect module for (fill-in-the-blank), wait until your hand feels a little heavy or tingly, then put your hand wherever on the body or in the field that it feels it needs to go - sometimes touching the body, sometimes not.

This may be over the solar plexus, or on the top of your head. Then ask for it to be installed and activated and request it runs until it's not needed any more.

You can add an instruction such as 'use as needed' or 'until no longer needed'. Putting one in a person's field for when they are ready for the information is also highly useful.

If you have difficulty feeling for the module, Dowse with your tongue for a YES signal for when it is ready.

The 'Doctor This' Module

I wanted to make up one module that would solve all the problems without having to continuously make up another and another. And so I was inspired to do this.

I make up a disc of light, downloaded all the morphic fields, information and personalities of healers, shamans, therapists of all kinds from the dawn of time till today. After I collected all the info, I installed the disc and that was it.

Later on when I checked it again, I was hit by a vision of thousands of closed doors that I felt to be representative of all the therapists categorizations and disciplines that I intended that would be always open and help each other. I uploaded the module for use by any and everyone.

To use this module, you can either download it or just point at your concern whatever it is and say : "Doctor This". Here is what usually happens when you use this, but not necessarily :

My cheeks felt very irritated due to my beard and sensitivity and I felt a strong urge to scratch them which is not a good thing, so I just said "Doctor this".

An image hit me of a line of doctors; each would come up with an approach, and I would feel it upon my cheeks. I was not surprised when it totally subsided.

I had pain in my left knee, and as I walked I said "Doctor This" and left it for a while. Suddenly it went away! Usually I see a line of crazy-ass doctors which is really hilarious!

Templates

Instead of forming a module in your hand, you can imagine a circle of Light on the floor (or wherever) and load it in the same way as a module. Then you can step into it, or send the circle of Light wherever it is needed.

At my Level 1 & 2 seminar I wanted to be better able to 'play like a child' - to improve my ability to visualize and create more interesting and fanciful ways to use ME.

So I made a circle of Light, loaded it with my desire, and then stepped into it.

I immediately felt a change.

Post Boxes

You can form and send a module of healing to another person (healee) who is far away. The process is a variation of making a module.

Ask your Heart to link to the Heart of the healee to identify the problems and their causes, and determine the correction that is needed for healing to occur, and then to have the required module (healing package) made and placed in a post box in front of you.

Imagine rows of post boxes in front of you, and then try to put your hand in each one to take out the package - one will be open, so take out the healing package.

Now throw it to the healee - saying "GO !", "INSTALL !", then "ACTIVATE !".

All this is very simple and easy to do; now check by Dowsing (or feeling if another box is open - another form of Dowsing) if a further healing package is needed - and if so send it to the healee in the same way.

One last major action for you to do - send your love, thanks, and gratitude to all who helped the healing package to be successful.

In some rare cases all boxes will be closed - for whatever reason the healing package is not available. In such a case, ask that a package of True Holy Love, Namaste be placed in a box. Then send it in the same way to the healee.

This will always be there, since it cannot ever cause harm and will always be beneficial.

Other Uses

This method can be used for other purposes, such as ensuring that a process (like selling a house) goes smoothly without any problems.

Send the requested module to all who are involved with the process (purchaser, seller, lawyers, mortgage companies, etc.) - and perhaps sending clones to supervise if your Heart suggests such action.

The module may include any aspect of space/time, and may even be used for inanimate objects.

You are only limited by your imagination!

Healing Yourself

Perhaps the hardest of all healing to accomplish is on one's own self. If using a Ptah Pendulum to make changes in your own aura, or to pull unwanted energies from your head or body, you are limited by the extent of your reach.

To overcome this, use a token such as a doll or teddy bear; all you have to do is rotate your Pendulum clockwise over the token saying "Let this wonderful Teddy Bear now represent (your name) who was born (place and your date of birth) now located at (present place)" - and your Pendulum will continue to rotate clockwise to indicate that the token now represents you.

Of course, this method also can be used to manifest distant healing on a person thousands of miles away.

Hold your Ptah Pendulum over the head of the token, and ask that all non-beneficial energies be removed from all the auras of the person, and be taken to be healed and in their rightful place. Your Pendulum will first circle clockwise to put love where it is needed, then anti-clockwise to do the extraction, and then clockwise again to replace the extracted energies with love.

When that spot has been cleared, expect your Pendulum to swing towards another place where there are unwanted energies, and to repeat the clearing and healing process.

When your Pendulum stays still, it indicates that all aspects relative to the vertical position have been cleared.

Next place the token on its back, and repeat for energies in that plane; when finished, turn it onto its front and repeat the process, so that all unwanted energies in the plane relative to the back of the person are also cleared.

After clearing the auras, you may be guided to pull out stuff with your etheric hands, or to use the 2-Point method to do further healing.

You will find that using the tongue signals explained in Chapter 4 are most useful to check "Is the clockwise (or anti-clockwise) rotation finished?", "Is anything to be pulled out?", and then request that your Heart-Mind-Brain team place your hands where they are needed to do the required work.

If your are unsure at any point, ask "If I knew what to do next, what would the correct answer be?"

When you ask clear and precise questions, you will receive the answer in some format that makes sense to you. Remember that you are not the healer, but just a conduit for the Angelic Beings to manifest the healing.

Chapter 15 *Telling Each Other what we Do Helps us both do Healing True*

Odds and Godsends

Note: *This chapter comprises hints and comments from friends. The typefaces vary - to indicate different friends.*

I have recently had some experiences where the universe/ source is playing with me. Computer/phones working - not working - working, etc.

Plus my husband's cell phone disappeared. We both were pretty sure where/when it was least seen. We searched everywhere. So a friend told me it was there, but in another reality and to ask for it to come back to THIS reality. I did that and it showed up in the bedroom closet. The funny thing was it didn't show up in the exact place it was left, but one story up !

I suspect the lost item showed up in a different location, at least in part, so that I might notice I was having a "Toto, this is not Kansas anymore" experience.

We have had several lost items with similar outcomes.

Sometimes it involves a game of the Fairies borrowing stuff. When we ask nicely, the lost item shows up again, but NEVER in any place where we might have actually left it.

Theta Healing

I would like to share with you something that I have been doing recently with which I am having some great results. In Theta healing (for those who don't know) one of the aspects of the system is belief digging - muscle testing for a particular belief and then 'digging' all the way down to the base belief of which the original belief was stacked upon.

By clearing the correct base belief you are not only collapsing the top and bottom belief but all other belief stacks/trails that feed off of the original base belief. Clearing the subconscious limiting beliefs will change your perception of reality.

You also have 4 levels of the subconscious in which belief programs can be stored - Core, Soul, Genetic and History.

When doing the process for clearing the beliefs you need to do a mini-meditation where you go all the way up to the 7th plane and ask creator/god to change the given negative belief into the correct positive replacement. If the belief exists on more than one level then the program needs replacing individually on each level. You then take your consciousness down to the client and witness the healing occurring.

The whole process takes a minute or two per belief but does speed up after your know how to form the wordings properly etc. However you can break the whole process down in the terms that ME uses and do the whole process instantly.

1. <u>Place your intent:</u> To find the base belief that needs changing by the process of digging.
2. <u>Make your first point:</u> Find the place on or off the body where the belief is stored.
3. <u>Make second point:</u> Find the place on or off the body where the highest and best replacement belief exists - or simply use the field of the 'creator' or the '7th plane'.
4. <u>Feel or see a connection </u>between the two and drop down/ release it into the field and feel the shift.

Now check using muscle testing etc to see that the base belief and all other beliefs which where stemmed from it have now been cleared.

Using muscle testing you may find a subconscious 'fear of affection'

- which is formed from a 'fear of showing my feelings'
- formed from the 'fear of revealing my identity'
- formed from the belief "if I reveal my identity I will lose everything I worked on" (probably from a past life)

- formed from "If I lose everything I worked on then I will have wasted time" formed from "There is not enough time to waste'"
- formed from "Wasting time means I may die without experiencing everything I wanted to"
- formed from the base belief of "I am afraid of death"

In an ideal situation (may require more digging) the base belief of "I am afraid of death" is essentially the cause of all of the above fears/beliefs including the original "fear of affection". By replacing the base belief with correct highest and best replacement belief plucked from the field of the 7th Plane etc. all other beliefs stacked on top of "I am afraid of death" have now been cleared. I also find that doing it this way clears the belief automatically on all levels at the same time without conscious effort.

Have a try and see if it works for you

Star of the Heart

Set up the symbol generally known as the 'Star of David' within your body, such as the points are the forehead, shoulders, hips, and groin.

The center of the star is your heart. Within the heart place an intent. Then you can make the star spin, as in the Merkaba meditation. Spin the star, and as it spins, it becomes smaller and smaller. Then see the star spinning out of your body, to a point about three feet away from you. You can now send the small spinning star out and insert it into a situation, person, place, etc.

The second technique is to imagine that you are transferring your senses to the star, such as sight, hearing, etc.

When you feel right, send the star to a 'location', and remote view, or remote influence. This is a form of 'astral travel'.

For centuries, mystics and shamans have left their physical bodies to explore higher planes of consciousness in the astral worlds.

Many people have glimpsed these realms through dreams, illness, or spontaneous awakenings. Astral travel or astral projection is a shift in your reference point, or a change in shifting from one state of consciousness to another. It involves changing your point of reference, as in Einstein's Theory of Relativity; many observations are changed by changing the 'measuring' or observation point of reference. It is this lifting of the 'energy body' in to different realms of consciousness and returning with the memory of what as taken place.

Astral projection is the actual bi-location of the physical body at one place and the 'energy' body in another. The difference is that one's consciousness is transferred to that 'energy' body.

When the 'energy' body returns, the journey is remembered by the degree of continuity of consciousness the traveler has developed. Astral projection is used to gather knowledge.

For example, this is also the 'middle world'. This is the spiritual dimension of our physical world. It is where the Native American scouts went to see the real lay of the land, for hunting and protection of the tribes. Astral Travel in the middle world is in present time.

You can simply go to your inner star, see a path there straight out in front of you, and travel it, with a clear intention and purpose for your journey.

Another way is to travel this pathway, arrive at a portal, enter the portal by turning right, as if you were to walk though a doorway and turn right to continue your journey.

Remote Viewing, another term for Astral travel, is a matter of mentally projecting to another person or a distant location and observing with your inner eyes what is taking place there, what your target person is doing and/or details of the distant location. Your mental consciousness is just extended to that distant location.

<u>To perform Remote Viewing</u>: Once you're relaxed and are at ease in your star, begin to visualize the person you'd like to view (or the location desired to see). Capture their essence in your mind - how they look, how they move, the sound of their voice, everything. Then if you want to connect, as you walk through the portal door turning right, say, "I now want to perceive information about where (name of person or location) is, what he's doing, how he's feeling, etc." Be open to everything that comes in - every thought, feeling and emotion.

To return, go to the portal door again, and pass through it turning left.

Another method for doing this is to just envision that when inside your star, your environment is slowly changing and becoming exactly like the area where you want to travel, or that the star just changes the landscape to who and where the person is that you want to visit.

Another technique that one can use on time travel journeys is the use to the Time Device. Simply imagine that the palm of your left hand is the face of a clock, with a date readout. Mentally take the index finger of your right hand, point it at the open left hand clock date and set the desired time and date by rotating the index finger of the right hand one revolution per desired time increment. For example to advance ten units of time rotate the face of the clock ten times clock wise. To go in to the past ten units of time, rotate the face of the device ten rotations counter-clockwise.

I love, love LOVE taking people's organs out and throwing them in tanks. Since doing so, I've noticed a mix of the other M.E. levels.

My favorite example is I was playing with someone's lungs and a Richard Bartlett archetype steps in. He was wearing an illusionist's outfit (black tux looking thing with a red slash). He started doing magic tricks, throwing gold sparkly energy and flaming hoops around the tank and what not. My attention turns away for a moment, and when I look back, he's taken the Lungs out of the tank and is blowing them up like a balloon. This entertained the shit out of me, and I managed to get them away from him before he tied them into animal balloons. The Health Meter indicated strong and a done window appeared. Looking back through the notes, I notice the 'Energy Leakage' protocol and think the RB archetype was doing that.

Another thing I've noticed is elementals and frequencies are starting to step in when I play with the star. I've chosen the Traditional Chinese Medicine route with this sucker and play within those rule sets. Sometimes when I get a hit, say Metal, a salamander appears over fire, slides down the star and a tornado erupts. The star shakes with all these colors and a 'Done' window has appeared.

In short, the more I'm playing with M.E. Level IV, the more things from M.E. Level's I, II and III are coming out to play.

Screen Work

I have a thing I have been using in lieu of a classic 2-Point that is working like mad for me. It is not in lieu of actually, it is just another way to view and play with a 2-Point.

You picture a large computer screen in front of you, with two windows open, lined up right next to each other.

Window one on the left, has your current reality. Window two on the right, is the reality where what you want is happening.

All you do at this point, is dissolve or erase the frame on the windows that abut each other, then the two become one.

It just showed up one day and I have been using it ever since.

Note: The Silva method has a similar technique.

"You have to play with it and see how it works for you. I rarely have a desired outcome in mind. If you only use M.E. to manifest what you specifically intend, then you limit it to being able to provide only something that you can imagine. This prevents or limits something BETTER than you can imagine from showing up".

Let's take money for an example. When I 2-Point my finances, I place the energetic pattern of my finances in front of me. I simply intend that to happen, and I often see it as a pattern.

Trusting that the pattern is in front of you, whether you can imagine it or not, is what's important. Doing M.E. is all about trust - the more you trust, the more powerful you are.

Knowing that the pattern is in front of me, I reach out (usually physically with my hands) and find a point in the pattern that feels stuck, hard, rigid, or different.

Then I search for a second point in the pattern that intensifies the feeling in the second one so that I sense that the two points are connected.

Then I drop down and let the two points change into a more useful state, one that feels better than how they were at first.

This process has shown to correspond to healthier, more abundant finances. I don't know (and don't need to know) how this occurs. It may be beyond my comprehension. The more I do not know, the more powerful it seems to be. The more important thing is to develop an attitude of trust.

Address Information - NOT problem!

Several days ago, I was playing with a group of others. I was suffering from root chakra 'stuff' - really painful and intense. I put out the intention to clear all the uncomfortable stuff I was feeling. We put that on the clipboard. The individual I was working with began working NEVER EVER addressing the dozens of trauma's that were in the root chakra. The information was showing up to the left of my head.

"In M.E. we don't address the problem, we observe the information".

After a 2-Point and a time travel, all of a sudden, all root chakra stuff was gone and it became a headache on the left side. In the past, I would never be able to clear that much root chakra stuff without running energy or a bunch of other techniques.

I could guarantee that there were multiple patterns down there that had to be addressed if we would have taken the time to muscle test it.

We could have cleared it with some other technology but it would have been very time consuming.

In the past, I would have 2-Pointed my root chakra and it would work after sometime. But by focusing solely on the information, and not root chakra, we were able to instantaneously transform it.

I then indicated that now we were working on a headache. All of a sudden the entire morphic field that I had called root chakra stuff had moved from root to head which was where the information was showing up in the first place. A time-travel, a parallel universe later, it was gone. And we asked: "Is the healing complete ?" YES.

It is so easy especially if we've been programmed with other healing modalities to get suckered back into time and space (and more difficult routes) by not paying attention to the information. It is part of our programming that we are learning to give up. And the tendency is to revert back to something that we know.

I suggest not to follow that urging and at least continue to play in the matrix before you decide that chakra's are real. You will get results but you are defeating the purpose of ME.

If I have an illness I want to shoo away, I go into altered consciousness, with my intent (the left brain intention) then I go into my mental screen and project this desire there.

This desire came from intent. Feeling is built-in in the desire (right brain feeling intention).

I stay there in my screen and construct my picture of wholeness, my desired result; when done, I breathe out and drop into my chest. I know it is manifested.

I just did this the other day. I woke up with the most intense right leg cramps. I twisted this leg round and around until the cramps subsided. All day long, there was so much pain that I was hobbling. So I did this procedure and ... voila ... in a couple of hours, it was as good as new - not instantaneous this time, but it works.

Spoon Bending

I've tried bending a metal spoon several times before by doing clearing statements, intentions, etc. but it never worked.

Today I set the intention, did some clearings, and when again it did not work I did a 2-Point while looking at the area where I wanted it to bend and then said "now" - and sure enough it bent easily.

Installing a Vibrational Meter

Drop down to Heart Space. Visualize a vertical 'thermometer' of Vibrations rating from 0-1000, 1000 being the highest vibration. Ask yourself: "If my Vibrational state could be measured, what would it be ?"

Mine showed up halfway- about 500. Visualize a lever on the meter and push that lever UP... UP... UP....

Notice what you feel. Install. Activate. Run. You can add or tweak this module if you like.

Friends felt a definite change or shift in their feeling/ vibrational state. We are now checking our vibration-state during the day and night and pushing the lever UP when we feel it is not at optimum level. What we have noticed is that no one so far has been able to get their lever up to 1,000. Interesting....

I am feeling sad right now and anxious but I tried this again as the module has settled. Again it started at 750 and I pressed the lever up and it went to 900 where it was 850 before. Going for 10,000 !

We discovered that with some major clearing of 'not useful' patterns, some major shifts occur and higher vibrational states can be obtained. We are reaching for higher vibrational states with this template.

Teaching Son

I have wanted to start teaching my 10 year old son to play in the sandbox that is his life. I decided one of the first steps was to teach him intuition. So I picked 3 dixie cups and played hide the silly putty ball.

To keep him interested I told him if he got it on the first try he would get a $1 and if he got it the second time $.50.

First try he overthought it and took 3 guesses. Second set of three got it on number 2, third set he got it on 1st try, fourth set I set out 6 total cups and he nailed it on the first try. I realized I would soon be a poor man if I let him continue to play for money.

I kept coaching him to be in heart space when guessing. What a beautiful thing to teach trust. When he set up the 6 cups to see if his Dad could do it, I ran my hand over the 6 cups and waited for the shift; whoa, surfed the same wave I was riding in Seattle at the ME seminar. Not quite as fast as my son, but nailed it none-the-less.

Creating Your Field of Dreams

1. Build It And He Will Come

Your life reflects your state of consciousness. You must build the state of consciousness that reflects your highest dreams. They must be dreams build on love, not on fear. You MUST be honest with yourself why you want what you want - in the end people wish they had loved more.

In the movie 'Field of Dreams', it was a dream in which the entire purpose of the voices' instructions was to lead him to the moment of great healing.

You must listen to the guidance of the universe. It is always there.

Sometimes it's through symbols and sometimes through inner knowingness. You must build your state of consciousness to hear it's voice.

2. Go the Distance.

You must be willing to pursue your dream despite any obstacles that present themselves. Thomas Edison failed 9000 times before he invented the light bulb. Steven

Speilberg dropped out of junior high school; when he returned, he was placed in a learning disabled class. Einstein's parents thought he was mentally retarded and his teachers told him he'd never amount to anything. They all overcame these negative morphic fields. Do not make excuses for your difficulty with M.E. or anything else. Just keep persisting.

De-Labeling for Change

I was playing around with observation lately and I realized that it all felt much more complicated than it really is. So I thought I'd share some of my discoveries. ME is basically the art of change through observation; let us see how powerful is observation through a very simple exercise.

Remember a time when you felt very happy, sad, angry, euphoric, excited, tired, etc.

Then start observing this e-motion. Try to describe to yourself the boundaries that are keeping the stream of that emotion intact in all of your 5 senses.

De-label the emotion completely - happy, feels good, etc. to blank.

Now see the energy within the boundaries and the boundaries themselves all as energy.

Now see the rest of your body and all of your surroundings also as energy.

Notice the instant shift when you do so - feeling lighter, vaster, happier, euphoric, etc.

Basically you've dematerialized that emotion through de-labeling and seeing it as it truly is (Energy) without any polarity.

Now do the same again, but after de-labeling the emotion/pain/thought/etc. label it again and define it. Feel how it materializes when you do so, then de-label it again.

Do this several times until you start to get a feel for how a belief/emotion/thought/etc. materialized and dematerialized - this is Quantum Mechanics at hand.

This should show you that you have been doing it unintentionally all the time since you were a baby - through social conditioning .

Now try and do this with all of your beliefs and test to see what happens. After all there's no risk - as you know to materialize it back if needed.

Releasing Unwanted Patterns

I've been using M.E. very successfully in releasing energetic patterns such as old programming, sexual abuse, relationship, lineage, etc. First I see if it's being fed by the collective; if so, I clip it free (fingers as scissors, no problem), then find out where it came from.

Sometimes the client created it at a earlier age, but often it comes in through the lineage - especially generational issues such as sexual abuse patterns, scarcity, fear of others, intimacy - practically anything. Then find the pattern by counting back generations. Once I've found the energy pattern I send it to the Matrix with these instructions: "Release this to the quantum field to be completely neutralized". This way, there's no 'garbage' being sent out, instead, the original energy is completely neutralized. Often I bring back some of the neutralized energy to the client with specific intent that supports/ empowers them in a way they would like.

I can't tell you the layers of energy that get lifted, particularly in abuse situations. One client was pretty clear from her content after 15 years of therapy, shaman, and energy work. The pattern went back on both Mom and Dad's sides thousands of generations.

After the session she looked completely different - pure presence. She said she could tell, energetically, that she was finally free.

I was having a lot of trouble releasing certain old patterns in myself - which I experienced and perceived as strong generational patterns. Finally, it came to me to go into the 'Heart-space'. Then I took a BIG eraser and massively erased the negative emotions and patterns I had been struggling with for quite some time.

They had been presenting to me as very deeply lodged, generational family patterns going back a long time. Of course, that's only how I was viewing/perceiving them. They aren't really that. That was how I had created them to appear in my hologram.

That is why they can be erased. The story about them isn't actually 'true', isn't actually 'real'. They are just what your consciousness is manifesting to you in your made-up universe in this moment. The story you tell yourself about it is what makes it seem real to you.

Wow! Worked like magic. Really shifted me. This happened a couple of days ago. Sometimes some are still coming up, so I erase some more. I love this because it's easy, quick, and simple, and I can do it with the intention of massive and lasting erasure. I also find it really satisfying to make big wide sweeps with the big eraser !

Stop trying to 'fix' 'deafness' or anything else. See non-hearing as an interesting manifestation of the person who is deaf.

Try sitting in Heart space and asking one or more of these questions and waiting to notice something:

- Is there a more useful pattern for this thing we call an ear?
- Is there a place where person X hears better than now?
- If I was to see something useful concerning this unhearing, what would I see?
- Is this deafness a useful thing for person X?
- Is there something more useful for person X?

Whatever you notice go with it, trust in the infinite - for me, the crazier the better! For me infinite means infinite - so deafness is just a finite thing which can be gone in an instant.

I have 2-Pointed my son's vision so he no longer needs glasses.

Working with Water

Many Shamans, use water to symbolize Mana. When they want to accumulate Mana for a particular purpose, they take deep breaths and visualize themselves as fountains filling up with water until they are overflowing.

We have all had the experience of being in a place when suddenly the cat hunches its back and begins hissing, or the dog suddenly looks up at 'nothing' and begins to howl.

The point is, if you ever feel that any area in which you are working in or living in is being permeated by someone sending a negative vibration, or being permeated by a bad thought from someone created a long time ago, here is one way that the Shaman can deal with it.

Water dispels any negative vibrations very rapidly. The water absorbs them, and within seconds, the area starts to clear.

Find a small bottle or glass of any color, use a M.E. frequency, clean the bottle thoroughly, and fill it with pure spring water.

Hold the bottle or glass, gently pressed against the navel, in your cupped hands, left hand on the bottom, right hand on the top. Now close your eyes and think the most beautiful thought you can, and pour the loving vibration of that thought into the water.

Imagine you are a fountain overflowing with this vibration, and that the vibration flows out from you from your left hand, into the water, and collected by your right hand, as you do some gentle deep breathing.

Remember, energy goes where the attention goes. In Hawaiian Shamanism, the navel is the symbolic center for body, mind, and spirit. It manifests on the physical plane.

This water, being 'magnetized', has a number of very valuable effects.

Take a little water and sprinkle it on a rug or any other object. If you feel that a room in the house has bad vibrations, say, due to a quarrel, sprinkle water around that room.

This water will act as a 'blotter', absorbing the negative energy caused by anger, resentment, etc.

You could simply slowly run some water from the kitchen tap, to dispel negative energies in the household area. The running water will absorb the negative vibrations and carry them 'down the drain'.

When sprinkling the water or spraying it in a fine mist, it absorbs the negative energies; then, when the water evaporates, it disperses the negative energy.

You can also use the water in a small spray bottle to spray on your self to dissipate negative forces from your aura.

It is interesting to see the use of water in religious ceremonies: Holy water to bless, Holy water to remove possessions, for baptism, etc. All are related to the ability of water to remove negative influences. What we are elaborating on is the point that human energies can be focused and used for the purpose of healing.

The main factor in charging the water is to have strong and clear visualization and imagination - have a strong mental image of the end result that you want. It is all that is necessary, provided that you have a strong and clear image of the end result that is desired.

When charging the water, Imagine the energy has the specific healing desires wanted.

While charging the water, see the water already charged, and see your self drinking it, and see the results desired as already achieved in you mind's eye.

You can then take this charged water and use like medicine, say take 2 tablespoons every eight hours, or use the water as a salve, and moisten an effected part of your body with it.

You can also improve medications with the charging water technique. This approach is to increase the effectiveness of the allopathic medication, for example, increasing the effectiveness of pain medication and canceling side effects that are not beneficial.

When charging the water, while imagining the energy flowing from hand to water to hand, include images of power when taking the drug. See an image of yourself becoming better, feel how it feels to feel better.

It helps to know in layman's terms how the drug works and to include these images in charging the water. For example, if one is taking a direuritic, use images of water flushing or draining out of the body.

One could then drink this water when taking the medication to help increase the effectiveness of the medication.

The charging technique can also be applied directly to the prescribed medication. Charge the medication, imagine the treatment of what the medication is supposed to do - while energizing the water, see the medication going into your system. Then see or imagine the positive results obtained with the medication. Then take the medication as prescribed.

For example, if your taking eye drops to help with cataracts, charge the bottle of the eye drop medication, seeing the cataracts dissolving and the vision as already clear.

From Dr. Emoto's work, who has written several books about how water can be altered and changed with intention, we are provided with factual evidence, that human vibrational energy, through words, ideas and music, affects the molecular structure of water.

Think of charging water in terms of vibration or waves of energy. It is easy to understand that language, the spoken word, has a vibration. Written words also have a vibration. Reading a novel can evoke various feelings and thoughts from the reader. The same with watching movies, where you now have language, visual symbols, with 'mood' music in the background of the scene. These are all symbols, which set up 'vibrations' in the subconscious mind.

Anything in existence has a vibration. The symbol of a cross would create the vibration of an equal arm cross -

not a crucifix, which has connotations of torture. So if one writes the letters L O V E, then these letters put out the vibration of love.

Water can then be imprinted with these vibrations. Positive words have harmonious clear vibrations. But negative words put out ugly, incoherent vibrations, which are called 'hookas' or heavy negative energies in the Andean Shamanic tradition.

Water has the quality of simply reflecting the energies and thoughts to which it is exposed. With this in mind, we can also 'charge' water to have the characteristics of a particular Power Animal or Medicine helper.

For example, find or draw the glyph for a bear. Attach the symbol to the water bottle or glass.

As you're charging it with the methods outlined above, rather than think of a specific outcome, which one could do, imagine the attributes of the 'Bear' medicine helpers that are in alignment with your desired outcome.

Bear Medicine is good for healing of physical emotional and mental problems, for introspection, gives one strength to overcome obstacles, and is a good symbol for protection.

What about applying these principles to bathing or showering ? What about 2-Pointing the water ? Why not Invoke a module and put it into the water ?

Splish, Splash - *the Saturday night bath may never be the same again !*

Easy World   http://www.iliveineasyworld.com

"I choose to live in Easy World where everything is easy."

Just say "This is so easy." It actually might seem to be hard but "This is so Easy" actually does make it easier.

When we are working only in our left brain rational mind our choices can be limited to what we already know or experience in our immediate environment. However if we breath--relax--allow our right brain and heart brain comes online.

We have access to more possibilities than our rational logical mind is aware of. We then enter the magical kingdom of EASY WORLD a reality where universal forces help us to get things done in an easier more effective fashion.

To pop into the EASY WORLD reality simply say "I choose to live in EASY WORLD" Then take the action step of BREATH-RELAX-ALLOW - and observe the magic unfold.

MIR-Method http://www.mirmethod.com

Say each sentence 3 times out loud while gently stroking your hand:

For Adults
1. Optimize acidity
2. Detox all toxicity
3. (a) Detach father;
   (b) Detach mother
4. Clear meridians
5. Supplement all shortages
6. Balance hormone system
7. Fulfill basic needs
8. Optimize Chakras & Aura
9. Clarify mission

Do twice daily for 4 weeks; if serious complaint, do 5 & 7 for 2 weeks, then 9 for 4 weeks.

For Kids
1. There is a little sun in my tummy.
2. That little sun is there to clean me.
3. I am now like a shining sun.
4. I see thousands of other lights around me.
5. Together we are a rainbow now.
6. I choose my very own colours.
7. My daddy has his own colours.
8. My mummy has her own colours.
9. I have my own colours.
10. My colours show me the way.
11. I hop from colour to colour.
12. And I end up on my own spot.

Quote: *"I did the MIR method last night before bedtime - as I was falling asleep I heard a weird noise (loud vibration/ buzz?). I had no idea what it was. At first I thought it might be the smoke alarm from one of the other apartments in the building. I wondered if I should get up out of bed but I was extremely drowsy and on the verge of sleep. Then I saw a large energy pattern traveling up and down my entire body very fast, it was two intertwined waves. I thought to myself - those wavy shapes look like the DNA pattern - and then I was asleep. When I got up this morning it occurred to me that the sound I heard was probably internal."*

Notes:

De-label the organ - don't call it a shoulder, but a collection of Energies doing a particular dance as lead by their leading Elemental. Link them to a better dance that they Love to do - this will then heal you!

Chapter 16

Healing with Love is an Art.
Best accomplished with your Heart.

Further Thoughts

The information that is in this book, and in the books of Richard Bartlett that you have read - as well as all similar sources of healing and other beneficial knowledge, have been absorbed into your sub-conscious data banks - probably holographically in every cell.

Your sub-conscious is like a fantastically fast and powerful computer - and action is based on memories stored there before your logical mind gets involved.

Whenever you re-read the books and do actual healing using the methods described, you are joining and boosting the M.E. morphic field, and re-inforcing these memories.

This is especially so when you work with others who have experience with M.E. - either at seminars or in other groups.

Your Heart Field in this context is not just your physical heart, but a combined field including all your Chakras and your Assemblage Beam.

The Assemblage Beam

The Assemblage Beam has a major influence on a person's personality and behaviour, and if not corrected may prevent any improvement.

The point of entry should be centered, and the angle of the beam should be at right angles to the body. Usually the centre is slightly higher in females (they are often more emotional) than in males. These are marked 'F' and 'M' on the diagram shown on the next page.

The beam itself, about 2 yards (or 2 metres) in length, must be straight, without bends, kinks, or twists, and should be of equal lengths back and front of the body. Entry below 'The Gap' indicates approaching death.

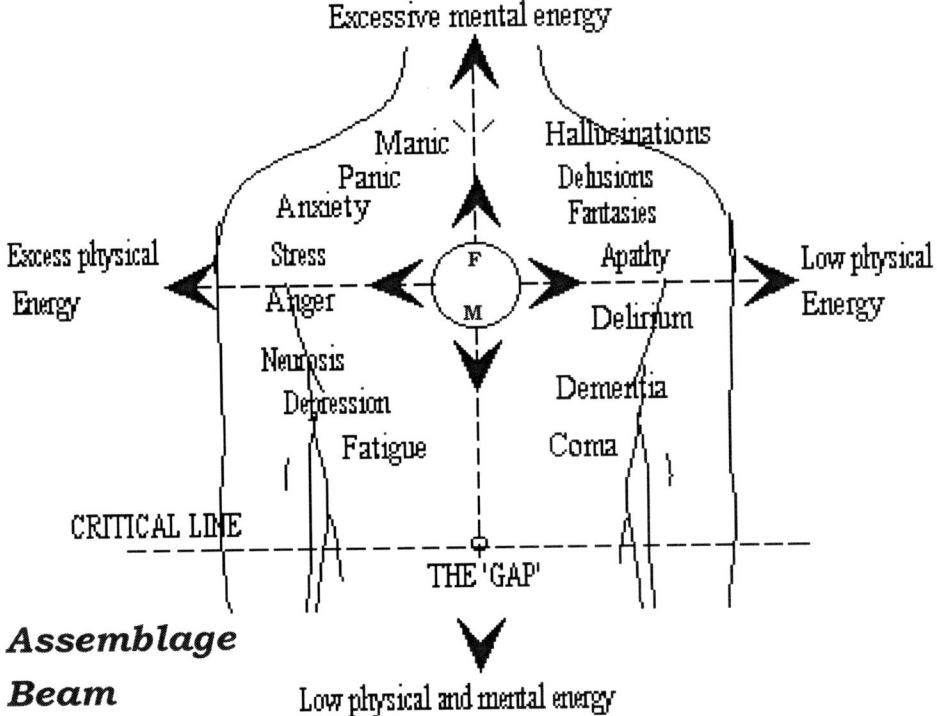

Excessive mental energy

Manic
Panic
Anxiety
Stress
Anger
Neurosis
Depression
Fatigue

F
M

Hallucinations
Delusions
Fantasies
Apathy
Delirium
Dementia
Coma

Excess physical Energy

Low physical Energy

CRITICAL LINE

THE 'GAP'

Assemblage Beam

Low physical and mental energy

The first person to publicize the Assemblage Point / Beam was Dr Jonathan Whale - in his excellent book 'The Catalyst of Power'; for more information see his website: www.whalemedical.com/ap1.html

Importance of the Heart Field

Your Heart itself has neurons, and seems to be very closely linked to your subconscious, which runs programs either automatically in case of perceived danger or as repeating actions which have become habitual, or which are called upon by your logical mind to do special tasks.

This is the case with M.E. work - you have built programs to help others to heal, and call them when needed.

One of the keys to success is to get the logical mind 'out of the way'. Another is to accept that you are not 'The Healer', but a conduit for healing.

The logical mind has a large part to play, however. It determines the identity of the healee, often gets involved in determining the problems of the healee and in deciding what action should be taken - and then checking if the healing has been successful and if more (even of a different aspect) is needed.

Things go far better when the logical and intuitive minds and brains are co-ordinated and work together as a team - especially if all the other parts of ones mind and brain (including ego) are part of this team.

I have found that when I place my awareness / consciousness above my head, enveloping them with golden white light, and then bringing them down on a count 7-6-5-4-3-2-1-0 to all my Chakras etc. it is a great help to get into such a co-ordinated Heart Field or Heart Space.

With practice this becomes a habitual co-ordination which is accepted as a habitual program by your subconscious, and is then run whenever needed - even without implementation by the logical mind.

Working with Your Heart

I have found that my Heart is my link to 'Upstairs' - all the metaphysical realms. If I ask a question, I rely on my heart to get the answer.

When I am Map Dowsing to advise people where to drill a well, I run my pencil along the boundaries of the land, asking my Heart to signal with my tongue when a water vein flows into the property. Having completed the boundary search, I ask my Heart to draw the water vein - and I get a squiggly line drawn on the map. I then ask the depth, low flow, and quality of the water, and mark these on the map.

It is also wise to ask if there is a Blind Spring on the land, where water comes from below and flows out in veins; if so, a person can drill into a vein, but never into the Blind Spring itself, since this would ruin it.

I understand that my Heart actually goes to the site and investigates all these points.

Some people open themselves to others in the Spiritual world to receive messages or do automatic writing; this can be very dangerous, since the Beings so contacted may not be beneficial. An alternative way is to ask your Heart to check out the Being, and if OK then to pass you the message or do the actual writing; thus any possible possession is avoided.

Metaphysical Realms

We are 'All the Same' - everything is made of the Tiny Baby Cosmic Energies doing dances in various teams to form different levels of 'Beingness' to form 'All that Is' - including 'All that is Not' in the physical world.

Because we are 'All the Same' we can communicate; more than that, we can use our Good God Energy to change the dances - especially to change dances that are having 'not good' results into becoming beneficial.

Blessing is a proven way of achieving this result - the best so far found is Blessing 995 & 885 with Healing 997 & 887, sent with 'True Holy Love, Namaste'.

There seems to be at least three major categories in the metaphysical realms:

Cosmic Field of undifferentiated cosmic energies, and communication matrices which make changes to the holographic fields, carry messages between stars, galaxies, universes, and distribute the 'Light of Life'.

This earth has its own matrices which carry emotions (anger, hate, greed, etc.) and other attributes (such as colours and energies) in grid lines set in the various metaphysical planes.

Morphic Fields which can be in many different places all at the same time, to which one can connect. It is possible that ArchAngels and Frequencies (as in Radionics and in M.E.) are morphic fields.

Note that a Frequency is a specific example of a vibrational pattern; these patterns have the same effect even if operating at different speeds such as those of sound, light, and thought. Essentially these patterns are the dances made by the Tiny Baby Cosmic Energies to take a form or accomplish a task, under the guidance of an elemental.

Thought forms of various types, such as clones, emotions, and thoughts of physical things - which appear as being real in the Astral Plane. Some religious figures may be in this category.

A major problem with all who are not in the physical plane is memory. These Beings have a very small active memory - so that they can remember their job and how to do it, and can access Akashic Records for long term memory.

They seem to lack any sort of medium term memory, and so have great trouble in working out problems - unlike human beings who have a logical mind-brain, store information in their body cells, and can hold a number of problems at the same time for processing.

So although all knowledge is available in the metaphysical realms, there is not much done with it; it is only when human beings access this knowledge that it is actually used.

Perhaps the final heaven desired by the Most High Beings is actually the physical world - if so, it is up to us to 'make it so'. This aspect is covered to a much greater degree in my proposed next book 'Elemental Creation'.

The more that you work with these morphic fields, Angelic Beings, and Frequencies the better is your subconscious able to record their abilities and how to access them.

This means that your subconscious does not have to remember how to do a healing in detail, but just how to get the needed help, working with your Heart Field.

It may be that some of these Beings will use human memory, working with the subconscious and Heart, to obtain the attributes of medium term memory and so be better able to do their own jobs - and get help from others to do the needed work.

Logical Mind-Brain Involvement

In most healing methods we are asking questions and using some sort of Dowsing, clairvoyance, or clairaudience to get answers.

In Radionics we feel for stickyness; in windows we feel for an opening; we visualize helpers or pictures representing problems as archetypes; we may be 'told' what action to take. All these are keeping our logical mind-brain involved with the healing process - not getting 'out of the way' as recommended.

Is there a way around this problem?

I believe that if we just have the intent to help others, then this can be done without deeper involvement.

When using Radionics we are relying on our Heart to obtain the correct answer; our Heart-Mind-Brain team then manipulates our nervous-muscular system to give a signal which indicates the answer - which we then decide to process in some special way.

If we can program our subconscious to work through our Heart-Mind-Brain team directly without our logical mind (ego?) being involved, then it will be quicker, involve less effort - and be more effective.

When I am healing with a person (distant or local) I ask my Heart to link to the Heart of the Healee, find what needs to be changed and how these changes are to be manifested, and then place my hands where they are needed (2 points - my Heart itself is the 3rd point) to manifest the change; my heart will relocate my hands as needed to effect further changes, until I get a 'completed' signal.

When I am doing Exorcism I rely completely on my Heart. I know that it can connect directly to the Heart of the healee to identify problems, with my subconscious to determine the help needed, and with the Angelic Beings and Healing Energies to get them to do whatever is necessary - all without my direct involvement. This is very important when exorcising the really dangerous possessing entities.

All that I do is run through a check list of work to be done, record the values obtained, and use EFT and M.E. techniques, and work with my Ptah Pendulum as directed by my Heart-Mind-Brain team.

All this is distant work - and just as effective as 'in person' since we are working in the metaphysical realms where time and distance do not matter.

In the same way I teach a very simple way of healing others at a distance:

Ask my Heart to link with the Heart of the Healee, to find out the problems as defined by the Heart of the healee, to identify the changes needed, to load a module to accomplish such changes, and to signal me when this is ready - then I throw the module to the healee saying "Go! Install! Activate!" Perhaps this saying could also be part of the programming.

I then ask my Heart if another module is needed for this aspect, and repeat if so; then I check if another aspect is to be worked on? Also checking if this is the right time, of course. Again, this could also be part of the programming.

Perhaps I am still too involved!

Would it be better just to ask my Heart to do all that is needed to make all the changes needed for the benefit of the healee, and just ask to be signaled if there is anything else that I should do?

At the end it is most important to send your Love, Thanks, and Gratitude to all who helped in the work, or as I personally do: "I send to all who helped in this work True Holy Love, Namaste, with my personal Love, Thanks, and Gratitude".

I use the 'Tongue Signal' almost all of the time - it is very quick and accurate: Roof of mouth YES, Jaw NO.

Healing Pain

If I get a pain anywhere in my body, I rotate the small end of my Ptah Pendulum clockwise over the painful spot to put in Love; when it stops rotating I reverse the ends and rotation to remove 'not good' energies and send them for healing; and when this movement ceases I repeat the first action - small end clockwise, to finish by putting in Love.

While doing this, I also rotate my awareness clockwise around the painful spot - and I usually hear 'clicks' in my head as changes are made. If the 'not good' were very strong, I may cough them out or expel them as spittle.

This also happens when I just use my awareness - for example when lying in bed, when it is difficult to use a Pendulum.

I use a similar method when doing distant healing on a token that represents a far away person (or represents me, since I can reach more distant and awkward places on a teddy bear - or a doll used for females.

Getting to Sleep

I use a double process to help me get a good night's sleep.
First, I tell all in my personal team (all that is in me):
"All in team (name) now relax, relax even more, relax deeperer and even more deeperer.
I/we release all toxins. I/we release all hurts, pains, suffering and afflictions - and all their causes.
I/we release all stress and tension - and all their causes.
I/we release all that is causing harm to our total Being - and all their causes.
I/we send all that is released to be healed with True Holy Love, Namaste, and to be in their rightful place.
I now have a really good refreshing sleep.
I wake up in the morning fit, strong, and healthy, full of energy and vitality, best able to do the work assigned.
I /we let it be so. I/we send our love and gratitude to all who so help us to be strong, fit, and healthy."

Second, I make certain that all the muscles in and around my mouth and eyes are fully relaxed.

As I inhale I think 'DEEP' and place my awareness in my Heart Space. As I exhale think 'SLEEP' and drag the 'chi'/'prana' from my Heart Space to the Chakra below my feet. I keep repeating this, gradually stopping the thinking but continuing the dragging - letting this be done by my sub-conscious mind.

Noxious Energies

All are the same cosmic energies in different configurations.

Key is locate, identify, heal. Most are due to water veins (carrying noxious energies to be healed), Curry grid (not seen by clairvoyants since may be in Buddhic plane), EMF which pollutes the Hartmann grid (otherwise this grid seems to be beneficial).

Sustained exposure to these (workplace, usual chair, bed) interferes with person's cells, canceling the correct orders and causing disease, such as cancer due to vortex reforming Vivaxis leaving intention for cells to multiply infinitely. X-rays also cause a similar vortex.

Prevent by moving bed, chair, out of range, and/or Blessing the energies and grid lines / water veins - all as detailed in booklet "Sleep Well, Be Healthy" based on Kathe Bachler's research.

Cure cancer: Speak to all the energies in your total Being "I love you all; all now re-align with my master cell, listen to and obey the Wisdom of my Being, the Wisdom of my Body" - repeat this 3 times. This re-aligns the cells to your correct Vivaxis, and causes those not able to be healed good to be discarded by your body. Cancer will return unless the causes are eliminated - see 'prevent' above.

Affirmations

Subconscious pays little attention to rational mind - so most affirmations are disregarded.

But it pays great attention to what others say ! So to get attention of subconscious speak as if another person is speaking as well:

"Joe Bloggs is now Healing Good";

"You, Joe Bloggs, are now Healing Good';

"I am now Healing Good";

"All in me are now Healing Good"

substituting for the name and healing (or change) needed. 'Now' should be used - not at some unspecified future time, which translates to 'sometime, never' !

Using ME and/or EFT (Emotional Freedom Techniques) is also advisable, and can handle much more and deeper problems.

Sing a Happy Song

Are you ever sad or depressed?

There are very simple cures!

Know that you cannot have conflicting emotions at the same time, so think of when you were really happy - without any recollection of anything that stopped that feeling.

If you need a stronger boost, sing a Happy Song!

I'm Happy, Happy, Happy all day long
I'm Happy, Happy, Happy singing this song.

I'm Happy, Happy, Happy the whole day through
I'm Happy, Happy, Happy sending Love to you.

I'm Happy, Happy, Happy as can be
I'm Happy, Happy, Happy singing merrily.

Add your own extra verses!

Kundalini

Caduceus of medicine: The caduceus is the symbol of medicine. The root meaning of medicine or medicate means attention, which is also the root of meditation. The caduceus is a winged staff, with two serpents, and is carried by the Greek god, Hermes, who is said to be the messenger of the Gods.

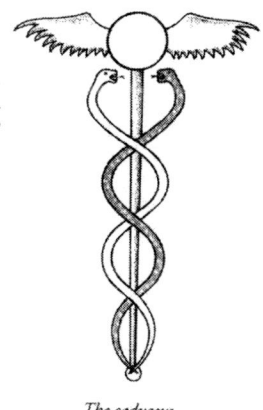

The caduceus

Together, Ida and Pingala form the snakes of the caduceus, while Sushumna forms the staff. The snakes intersect at the chakras.

At the ajna chakra, between the eyebrows, there are two petals, one on either side, just as there are two wings at the top of the caduceus. Thus, the caduceus is a symbol of the entire system of kundalini.

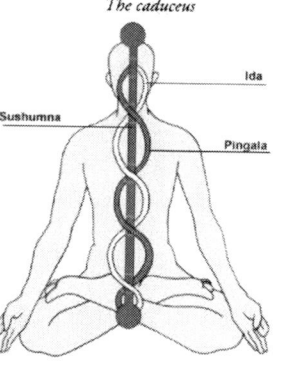

Ida is the left channel. Ida is white, feminine, intuition, cold, represents the . Originating in Muladhara, Ida ends up in the left nostril.

Pingala is the right channel. Pingala is red, masculine, logical, hot, represents the sun. Originating in Muladhara, Pingala ends up in the right nostril.

When I felt both the Ida and Pingala they seemed to go through the ear before circling to end at the other nostril.

Sushumna is the central channel.

Kundalini moves upwards running up the body from just below Muladhara chakra to Sahasrara chakra at the crown of the head.

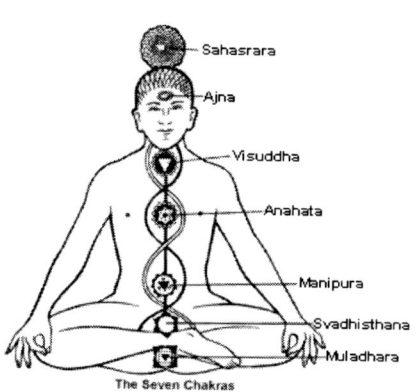

The Seven Chakras

According to the philosophy of Tantra Yoga, the entire universe is a manifestation of pure consciousness; the human being is a miniature universe. All that is found in the cosmos can be found within each individual.

Kundalini is an energy that exists in everyone's body, usually in a dormant state. This means that most people never feel it and never know it is there. But in a very few people, perhaps one in one thousand, this energy becomes aroused, activated.

This can be a happy event or it can be scary and disruptive, depending on whether you aroused your kundalini on purpose or by accident.

Benefits of Kundalini include intensified understanding and sensitivity: insight into ones own essence; deeper understanding of spiritual truths; exquisite awareness of ones environment; enlightenment experiences: direct knowing of a more expansive reality; transcendent awareness.

Some people report that they have a feeling that they are God; it is more likely that the 'God Energy' that is in all people has been activated in them.

Kundalini energy is not recognized by medical science, and is often little understood even among teachers of Yoga and meditative traditions. It is, however, mentioned extensively in the literature of Yoga. For most people kundalini arousal is at times pleasurable, sometimes intensely so, though it is at other times disruptive.

The kundalini, when awakened, moves from your coccyx where it resides at the base of your spine upwards. This explains the characteristic movements that result from kundalini arousal. These movements are typically in the pelvis and legs, in the mid back, and in the neck and head.

When it encounters barriers to its flow, it gets diverted and moves sideways into nerves and then muscles.

Disruptive kundalini causes an array of symptoms, which may include: insomnia or waking in the night; panic attacks; involuntary movements like shaking, twitching, arm waving, head tipping back, rocking or bouncing; enhanced perception such as in psychic phenomena; general bodily discomfort; the feeling that if you relax when the energy comes, it will get bigger and bigger and overwhelm you; inability to concentrate.

When a vertebrae is mis-aligned, causing the Kundalini energy to be blocked and diverted, it results in serious problems to meridians, nerves, and joints associated with that vertebrae.   Chiropractic help is needed!

Problems associated with Vertebrae

More than one vertebrae may be causing problems!

<u>Neck Region - Cervical Spine</u>

1C   Headaches, nervousness, insomnia, head colds, high blood pressure, migraines, nervous breakdowns, amnesia, chronic tiredness, dizziness.

2C   Sinus trouble, allergies, crossed eyes, deafness, eye troubles, earache, fainting.

3C   Neuralgia, neuritis, acne / pimples, eczema.

4C   Hay fever, catarrh, hearing loss, adenoids.

5C   Laryngitis, hoarseness, sore throat, quinsy.

6C   Stiff neck, pain in upper arm, tonsillitis, whooping cough, croup.

7C   Bursitis, colds, thyroid conditions.

<u>Mid-Back - Thoracic Spine</u>

1T   asthma, cough, difficult breathing, shortness of breath, pain in lower arms and hands.

2T   Functional heart / chest conditions.

3T   Bronchitis, pleurisy, pneumonia, congestion, 'flu.

4T   Gall bladder, jaundice, shingles.

5T   Liver, fevers, low blood pressure, anemia, poor circulation, arthritis.

6T　　Stomach problems / nervous indigestion, heartburn, dyspepsia.

7T　　Ulcers, gastritis.

8T　　Lowered resistance.

9T　　Allergies, hives.

10T　　Kidney problems, hardening of arteries, chronic tiredness, nephritis, pyelitis.

11T　　Acne, pimples, eczema, boils.

12T　　Rheumatism, gas pains, certain types of sterility.

Low Back - Lumbar Spine

1L　　Constipation, colitis, dysentery, diarrhea, some ruptures / hernias.

2L　　Cramps, difficult breathing, acidosis, ruptures/ hernias.

3L　　Bladder, menstrual (painful / irregular) problems miscarriages, bed wetting, impotency, 'change of life' symptoms, knee pains.

4L　　Sciatica, lumbago, urination problems, backaches.

5L　　Poor circulation in legs, swollen/weak ankles & arches, cold feet, weakness in legs, leg cramps.

Pelvis - Sacrum & Coccyx

Sacrum - spinal curvature.

Coccyx - Hemorrhoids, itching, pain when sitting.

Note: The nervous system controls and coordinates all organs and structures of the human body. Misalignments of spinal vertebrae and discs may cause irritation to the nervous system and so cause the problems listed above.

Healers such as Matrix Energeticists are prime targets for raising their Kundalini. I recommend getting an annual check-up from a Chiropractor.

One way to balance the Ida and Pingala is to breath in through one nostril and exhale through the other - then inhale through this last nostril and exhale through the first. Do this about 12 times, say twice a day.

You may be able to do this by using your awareness, but if you have any difficulty use your finger to close off the non-active nostril.

Level 4 Seminar Data

This book does not cover any of the Level 4 data - it is very complicated and hard to understand for most people.

I believe that all this healing work involves your Heart co-operating with the Heart of the person being healed, and that all the needed knowledge is available via the sub-conscious and the Matrix; hence the depth of involvement outlined in the Level 4 may not be needed, and if so it can be accessed by you linking to the morphic field, which includes all the Level 4 information - just ask "If I knew what to do next, what would the correct answer be?"

Then act according to the answer that you receive - remember that if you do not fully understand the answer you can ask more questions for clarification, as well s requesting your own Heart to place your hands, etc, where they are needed. Then check "Is any more work needed?" and if so, then ask more questions in a similar way.

'Into the Matrix' - CD set

This set of 6 CDs by Richard Bartlett and Melissa Joy Jonsson is excellent value - you can buy it on Amazon.

Each CD holds 1 session as indexed below:

Session 1 - 68 minutes
1. Introduction
2. Move into the grace of the moment
3. Co-creating a new possibility
4. Transcend your limitations
5. Slip siding away
6. Reacting v. responding
7. A different perceptual reference frame
8. Inner guide meditation
9. To be born again
10. Angels are watching me

Session 2 - 70 minutes
1. Introduction
2. The guides will flock to you
3. Trust, not faith
4. Tulpas and virtual reality
5. Beginning to hear your guides
6. The immateriality of the material world
7. Calibrating your guidance
8. Archetypes as guidance
9. No way as way
10. Grace is the vehicle
11. Silence and the presence of angels

Session 3 - 70 minutes
1. Introduction
2. Captain Kirk and the computer
3. At the heart of the matter is nothing
4. Exercise: Hearing the voice of your guides
5. Accessing your guides through the field of your heart
6. The eye is the centre of the cyclone
7. The heart as a point of no reference
8. Amplyfying love, appreciation, gratitude
9. Grace, the universal constant

Session 4 - 60 minutes
1. Introduction
2. Your unique bio-signature
3. Drawing information from the field
4. What you are is limitless potential
5. A portal into all that is
6. The folly of attempting to change
7. be in the world but not of it
8. A joyful masterpiece
9. Everything will deceive you except your heart

<u>Session 5 - 65 minutes</u>
1. Introduction
2. The heart is a spinning field
3. Virtual dolphins and universal joy
4. Becoming the totality of awareness
5. Directing your guides
6. Notice whatever you notice
7. There is no now
8. Infinite options available
9. The universe is playful
10. Strange forms of guidance

<u>Session 6 - 62 minutes</u>
1. Introduction
2. Accidents may be blessings
3. Universal consciousness knows itself through you
4. Story of the 9/11 fireman
5. The freedom of grace
6. Truth has a resonance
7. There are no mistakes
8. Become the message of your heart

Notes:

We all have 'God Energy' in us - and our task is to make it grow. This is like the parable of the tokens - do not hide it or misuse it, but expand it by helping all others in all creations, with unconditional True Holy Love, Namaste.

Appendix A   Forgiveness

If you have anger, jealousy, envy, hatred, resentment or seek revenge the 'then you' gave a part of your Spirit Consciousness the task of taking such action.

This part is now not able to operate in peace, harmony and love with the rest of your Spirit Consciousness and is probably going to attempt to hurt whoever is involved in this negative emotion.

Due to the law of attraction, it will bring similar fragments to you - and it is likely that you will be hurt, perhaps by attracting illness and disease associated with such emotional thoughts and feelings.

It is most important that you take all needed action to eradicate such thoughts, and so bring back any parts of your Spirit Consciousness so that all parts are again working together in peace, harmony, and love - preventing any potential fragmentation.

You need to forgive all who have ever caused you problems, ask forgiveness from all who you have thought of hurting, and also to forgive yourself - perhaps the hardest part of all!

It is most important that you successfully and completely forgive all who have ever caused you hurt or harm, forgiving from Soul and Spirit as well as mind.

This can be very difficult, especially in cases of abuse (or worse) by family members or those you trusted.

It is suggested that in such cases you accept that what was done occurred as a result of karma (or possession), and was not directly the fault of the perpetrators.

The key is to find some 'reason' to allow you to forgive, no matter how difficult this is for the rational mind. Failure to be so forgiving will prevent any exorcism from being effective - you may get short term relief, but problems will re-occur.

The following statement is to be considered carefully.

If acceptable, ask your "Wisdom of my Being, the Wisdom of my Body, my Heart, my sub-conscious, and all that are involved in any way, to align with Pure Heart and be correctly grounded, to accept and implement this intention with True Holy Love, Namaste, to be effective in all my life at all times and in all circumstances" and then read it aloud three times to make it fully effective. You must be honest and sincere!

"I [name], with True Holy Love, Namaste, do hereby forgive all who have caused hurts, harm, problems, and emotional, mental, and spiritual traumas to me and to all or any in my families, communities, and associations. I forgive you completely in all ways and in all aspects, in all planes of existence, in all domains, and in all dimensions. Whatever has been caused is now in the past and is of no importance to me now and does not matter to me any more. I am now free of all such causes and their effects."

"I [name] do humbly and sincerely apologize for all the hurts, harm, problems, and emotional, mental, and spiritual traumas that I have caused to all life forms, including all that were knowingly or unknowingly, intentionally or unintentionally caused, in all my life including all past lives of myself and all in my Soul families."

"I [name] do humbly and sincerely ask forgiveness for all the hurts, harm, problems, and emotional, mental, and spiritual traumas that I have caused to all life forms, including all that were knowingly or unknowingly, intentionally or unintentionally caused, in all my life including all past lives of myself and all in my Soul families."

"I [name] do humbly and sincerely ask Angelic help to Heal, clear, and remove from my total Being all emotional triggers attached or linked to my cellular, aural, and other memories of all these hurts, harm, problems, and traumas, and to keep me so free of non-beneficial emotional triggers in all nows and at all times."

"I [name], with True Holy Love, Namaste, do hereby bring back to me all Energies and Soul parts that have left me or been lost in any way, and do humbly and sincerely ask Angelic help to Heal them with Unconditional True Holy Love, Namaste, so that they can be in their rightful place".

"I [name], with True Holy Love, Namaste, do hereby release all non-beneficial Energies and Soul parts that have come to me in any way and for any reason, and do humbly and sincerely ask Angelic help to Heal them with Unconditional True Holy Love, Namaste, and take them to be in their rightful place".

"I [name] do humbly and sincerely send my Love, Gratitude, and Thanks with True Holy Love, Namaste, to all who so help and assist me in this forgiveness."

Life Review

There are many reports that when one dies you go through a review of your life. But since you are dead, you cannot make changes to this record.

If, however, you choose to go through your 'Life Review' whilst you are still in this world, you can take action to repair the results of what you did, and so remove any such negativity from your final 'Life Review' when you do die.

I did this, and it gave wonderful results in my present life.

If you decide to do this, go to our main web page: www.in2it.ca and then click on 'Life Review'.

The process may take a few nights, but it is very worthwhile!

Notes

Appendix B Entity Healing and Protection

It is understood that 'All That Is' (and all that 'Is Not') is the result of Tiny Baby Cosmic Energies doing different dances at different speeds in various planes of existence to form separate Beings who have different jobs.

The simplest dance teams could be called Lights, then Tinys and Smalls; perhaps these correspond to photons, electrons, sub-atomic particles - and so on.

Every Tiny Baby Cosmic Energy (and most of their simplest dance teams) Love, Feel, Think, and Act - they are Beings in their own right, and most want to have a good life helping others.

When they join a higher level team their energy, etc., is used by the leader of the team to do the job of the team; in some cases the leaders have been hurt, been given bad jobs to cause hurts, or are bosses who like to hurt others.

I am writing a book 'Elemental Creation' which goes into far more detail - but for our purpose here accept that there are healers in the 'True Holy Love Namaste' team who can dismantle such teams and will heal all who have been hurt.

This is similar to removing the bad high command of an army and assigning the soldiers to a different army - the 'Force for Good'.

The following procedures can be used to heal any entity (or group) that is attacking you - or other people.

They are even more powerful when done with a Pendulum to magnify their effects.

Simple Attack

If a person feels that they are under attack, a simple response is to locate and (if possible) identify the attacker.

This can be done by placing your awareness where the attack is felt, and then asking questions such as "If I knew The identity of the attacker, what would the correct answer be?"

Then speak in your mind to the attacker:
"I love you, all associated with you, and all that is in you all unconditionally, and send you Ho'oponopono with good God energy, Blessing 995 and 885, and Healing 997 and 887, all with this wonderful dream Namaste and True Holy Love Namaste itself; I send these to you extra, extra pure, extra, extra special, and extra, extra strong."

Severe Attack
I open with my Heart
In True Holy Love, Namaste
And that Love of Truth.

I send True Holy Love, Namaste
To the entity (*describe it by its actions*)
And to All Associated with you
And to All that are in each of you
Including All the Tiny Baby Cosmic Energies, Elementals,
And all their Families and Teams
I give you unconditional love.

I tell each and every one of you that I Love you more than I love myself.
But I do not like Bad Behaviour.

I send you all True Holy Love, Namaste
With Ho'oponopono.
With Good God Energy.
With Blessing 995 and 885 to help you in your path of life.
With Healing 997 and 887 including all Dances, Vibrational Patterns, Energies, Essences, Frequencies, and Fragrances that Heal Good in a Good Way with True Holy Love, Namaste.
With Ultra High Energy Howls and Lasers of Violet Light to Smash all defences against the Force for Good.
With Ultimate Light Dissolvers of All Negativity.
With the Wonderful Dream Namaste.
And with True Holy Love, Namaste itself.

I send these to all of you
Extra Extra Extra Extra Extra Extra Special
Extra Extra Extra Extra Extra Extra Pure
Extra Extra Extra Extra Extra Extra Strong

I send all this to you three times more
And three times more I send it to you all
And three times more I send to each and every one of you
True Holy Love, Namaste
With Ho'oponopono.
With Good God Energy.
With Blessing 995 and 885
With Healing 997 and 887
With Ultra High Energy Howls and Lasers of Violet Light to
Smash all defences against the Force for Good.
With Ultimate Light Dissolvers of All Negativity.
With the Wonderful Dream Namaste.
And with True Holy Love, Namaste itself.

I tell each and every one of you that I Love you more than I
love myself.
But I do not like Bad Behaviour.
I Ask each and every one of you
Do you Like to Hurt Others
Or Love to have a Good Life?
I Tell each and every one of you
Judge Yourselves NOW!

In our wonderful team Namaste
I / We place all our Trust.

Go now to be Healed with True Holy Love, Namaste, in
whatever way is best for All Creation.

*The result is that the energy / force of the bad entity is
taken away - and that of the Force for Good is increased.
This happens because the Tiny Baby Cosmic Energies (and
their families and teams) have 'changed sides'.
The Bad Controllers are now easily Healed in a similar
way.*

Clearing your Energy Field

You are responsible for maintaining your own energy field - this useful statement can help:

"I translate, transmute, transform, transfigure, release and repair all original causes, core beliefs and effects related to (*fill in the blank with what you want to clear*) replacing these with unconditional love; I do so throughout all time space and dimensional matrices both known or unknown. I declare it so and so it is. Thank you. I establish that my trigger point is my third eye. Whenever I touch my finger to my third eye I undertake and complete a deep clearing. I declare it is so. It is done. Thank you."

Deep Clearing

The 'deep clearing' is available at Tyhson Banighen's site:

http://energydetective.ca/2012/dowsing-2/deep-pendulum-clearing/

Preparing to Dowse

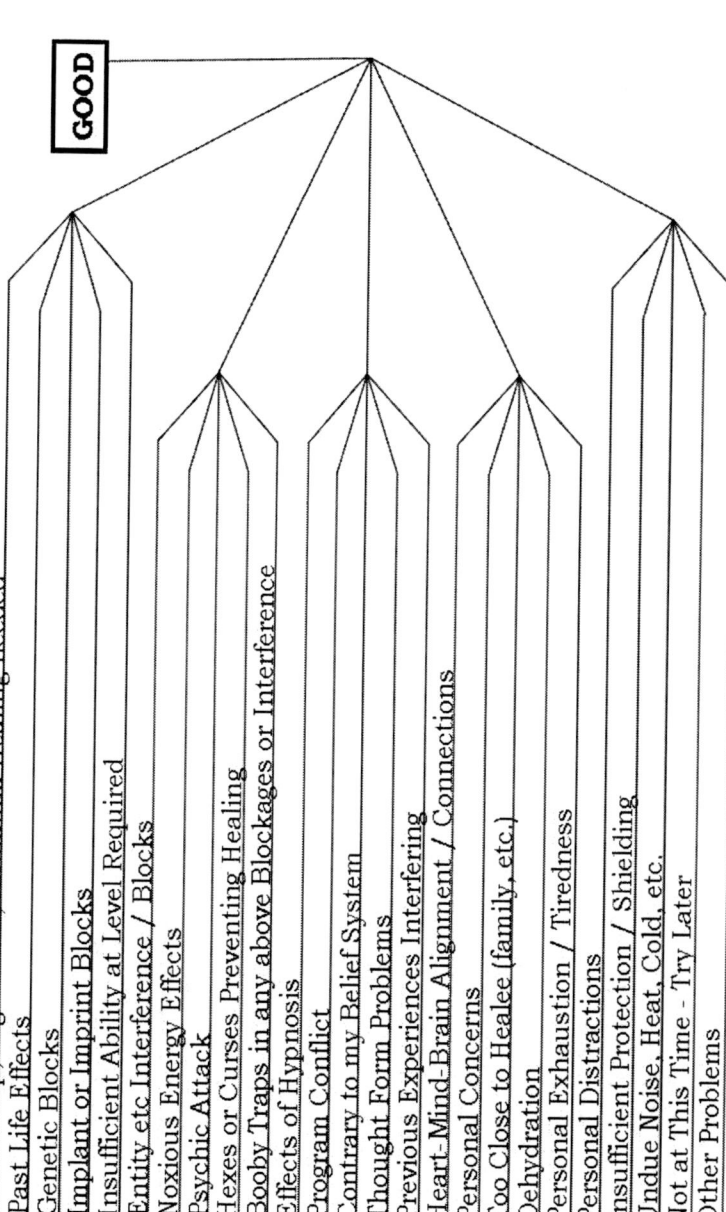

GOOD

Soul Group, Higher Self, Aumakua Healing needed
Past Life Effects
Genetic Blocks
Implant or Imprint Blocks
Insufficient Ability at Level Required
Entity etc Interference / Blocks
Noxious Energy Effects
Psychic Attack
Hexes or Curses Preventing Healing
Booby Traps in any above Blockages or Interference
Effects of Hypnosis
Program Conflict
Contrary to my Belief System
Thought Form Problems
Previous Experiences Interfering
Heart-Mind-Brain Alignment / Connections
Personal Concerns
Too Close to Healee (family, etc.)
Dehydration
Personal Exhaustion / Tiredness
Personal Distractions
Insufficient Protection / Shielding
Undue Noise, Heat, Cold, etc.
Not at This Time - Try Later
Other Problems

Your Handy Chart

Since most of us have two hands, we can use the spare one (the one not holding your Pendulum!) as a chart for many purposes.

It is best to use signals that conform to indicators that you see often, such as the speedometer and charging gauge of your car - your mind-brain team is accustomed to the signals used.

This is a quick way to check on your health or vitality, if medications are beneficial to you, how many tablets should be taken (dose, doses per day - these may change with effect already achieved), percentage accuracy of a statement, etc.

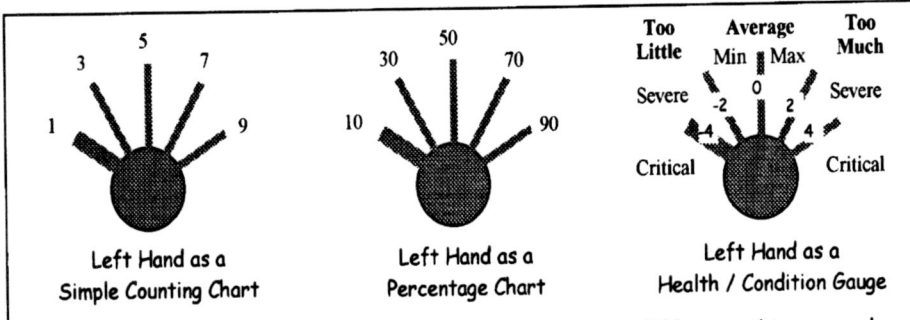

Left Hand as a Simple Counting Chart

Left Hand as a Percentage Chart

Left Hand as a Health / Condition Gauge

You can use your ingenuity to let your fingers mean many different things - so long as you have ensured that your Mind-Brain team understands the meanings to be signalled for each 'hand-chart' - and that you have specified to your Mind-Brain team which 'hand-chart' is being used for the Dowsing you are now doing !

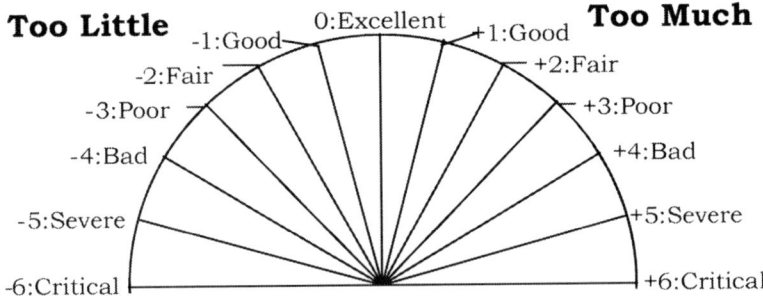

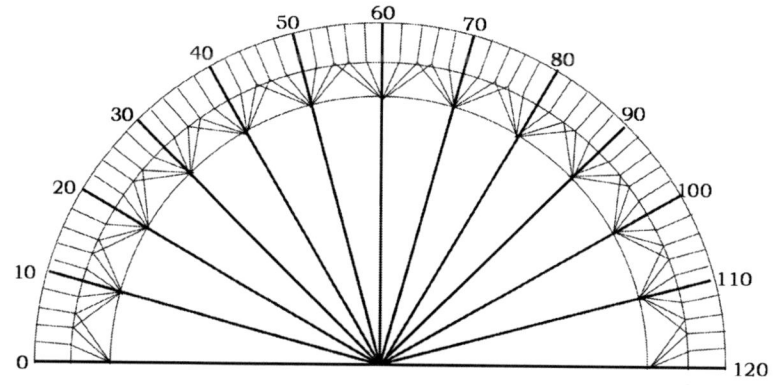

Percentage and Counting Chart

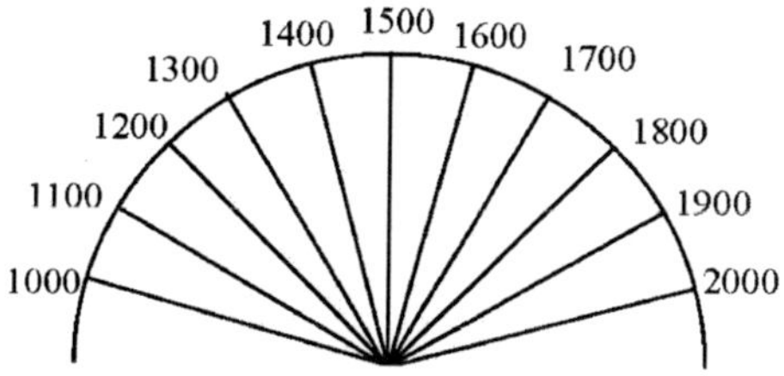

Soul & Group Past Lives

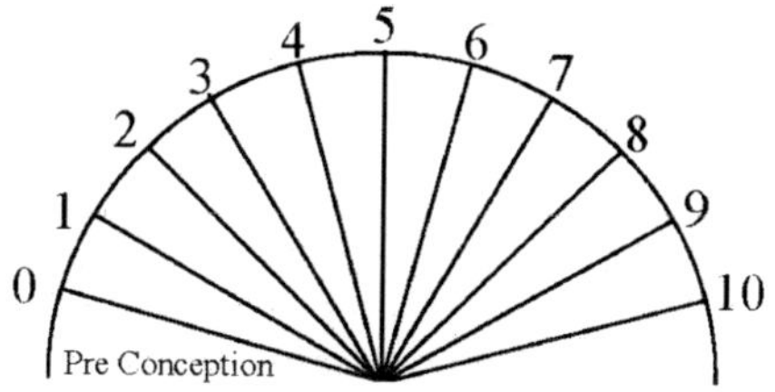

Months of Pregnancy

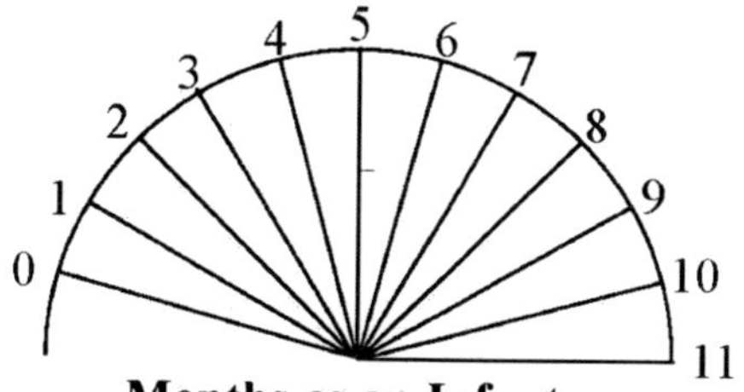

Pre Conception

Months as an Infant

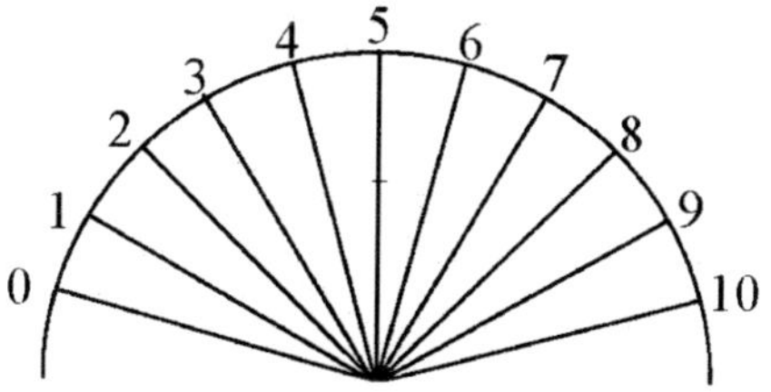

Age in Years as a Child

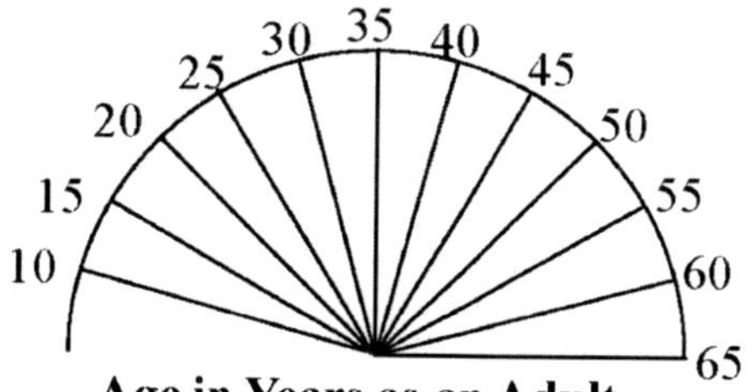

Age in Years as an Adult

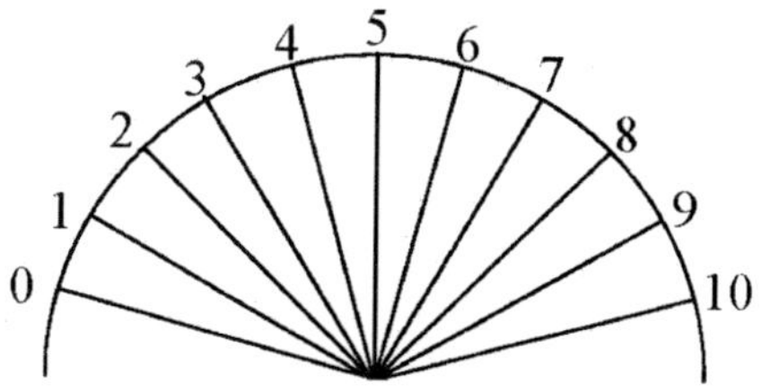

Seriousness of Problem

START

DONE

DONE

Blank Chart for your own use - 50 entries
More charts : www.in2it.ca/HealManual.pdf

Appendix D

Books published by the Holistic Intuition Society

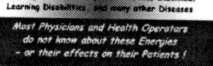

Earth Radiation

The classic record of Käthe Bachler's research into noxious energies involving 11,000 people in more than 3,000 homes and work places in 14 countries. 'Further Thoughts' by John Living.

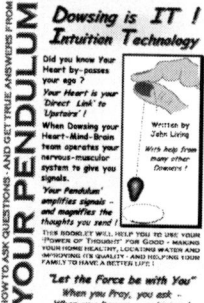

Sleep Well, Be Healthy

A concise summary based on 'Earth Radiation' designed as a booklet for distribution by Dowsers and Health Professionals aware of such noxious energies. Bulk orders for booklets, or buy the E-Book first to have a look at it.

Your Pendulum

Booklet with a glass bead Pendulum - designed as an 'Xmas stocking stuffer' to help people to learn about Dowsing - and how Dowsing can help them (and others). Excellent concise instructions. Bulk orders for booklets, or buy the E-Book first to have a look at it.

Intuition 'On Demand'

We all have Intuition - but many have problems getting help when needed. This book explains how you can do just that ! This book is 'entry level' - for people who are not experts !

Intuition Technology

Dowsing is 'IT' - an in-depth look at understanding ourselves and our environment, full instructions on improving our Dowsing abilities, and advanced knowledge about our total energy bodies and how we can work with the energies to improve health.
This book includes almost all of "Intuition On Demand" !

Vibrational Energy Healing

By the recognized Master Healer Bill Ellis - who gives hints for using a Pendulum for Healing, explains improvements made by Bill to many Healing modalities, and introduces some completely new methods of Healing - both for using 'Hands On' procedures and for distant Healing.   John Living edited this book.

Holistic Exorcism

It is estimated that over 70% of people are subjected to Spirit Possession - most people being completely unaware of infestation ! Most results from Spirit Fragmentation - in your past lives, childhood; death of relatives or friends; exposure in accidents, hospitals. Based on the experience of masters, it covers aspects unknown to most 'exorcists'.

Book to be published in Fall of 2013

Elemental Creation

An unusual look at how the various planes developed, how they interface in the physical and other dimensions, and how human beings can influence all of creation.

Buy 'Your Pendulum' & 'Sleep Well, Be Healthy' in bulk !

Lightning Source UK Ltd.
Milton Keynes UK
UKOW040137130413

209175UK00001B/99/P